Trans-Scalar Healing

Holistic Healing For Self, Others and Gaia

Howard F. Batie

It is good to be a seeker,
But sooner or later you must be a finder.
And then it is good to give what you have found,
A gift into the World for whoever will accept it.

Richard Bach in,
Jonathan Livingston Seagull

First Edition, (November, 2017)
Copyright © 2017 Howard F. Batie
All Rights Reserved
ISBN-13: 978-1978370548
ISBN-10: 1978370547
CreateSpace Independent Publishing Platform,
North Charleston, SC 29406, USA

Table of Contents

Chapter 4 –Trans-Scalar Healing

Acknowledgements

During my lifetime, I have met many people who have provided me with an opportunity to learn from them in one way or another, and I feel very blessed that along the way I have met many Life Teachers. First and foremost, among those who have enriched my life is my wonderful wife, companion and friend, Anita, who has taught me what true loving compassion and caring for others is. Her patience and wise counsel during the preparation of this and my other books has been a wonderful gift most deeply appreciated.

The development of this book could not have occurred without the constant support and encouragement of each of the members of my monthly Spiritual Discussion Group. These spiritually oriented friends have never failed to eagerly volunteer as I experimented with additional new techniques and processes that might serve to expand their day-to-day awareness into higher dimensions of consciousness. To each of you – a huge "Thank You!"

In particular, I thank Ronna Herman (www.ronnastar.com), who channeled the wisdom of Archangel Michael and his Infinity Breath Meditation, which has been adapted as a key element for energetic preparation of the healing practitioner. I also thank Greg McHugh (www.gregmchugh.com), a Certified Clinical Hypnotherapist in the Denver, CO area, for permission to adapt his "White Light Angel Healing Process" in support of the healing processes in The Temple Of Healing.

A very special "Thank you" is also given to the gracious and selfless channels in my Spiritual Research Group who have supported me in gathering and editing the information received for the many Spiritual Journeys we have taken together in support of this and my previous books: Kayla, Sandy, Karen, Leigh, Sylvia, Veronica and Dee (all pseudonyms) – I thank you all from the bottom of my heart.

And to my Spirit Guide and Higher Self, as well as the many additional spiritual beings in the higher realms of existence with whom I have been able to consciously experience their love and wisdom, especially Archangel Michael, Ascended Master St. Germain, and Ascended Lady Master Kwan Yin, I acknowledge and recognize your assistance, guidance, and yes, even your occasional proddings as I began to open my eyes to the real reason I'm here on this planet now. I send deep love and gratitude for all your compassionate patience and wisdom in guiding the creation of this book.

Introduction

Background. When I was about 9 or 10 years old, my parents, my two younger brothers and I piled in Dad's 1938 Chevy and drove north to my Grandparent's house in Seattle, Washington where many additional aunts, uncles and cousins had gathered for the Thanksgiving holidays with all the turkey, stuffing and gravy we had been looking forward to for several months. The pre-Interstate four-hour trip of nearly 100 miles took us through the many narrow back roads and small towns, but we finally arrived and ran into their home just as "Gramma" took the last tray of deliciously-smelling gingerbread-men cookies out of the oven. Funny how she always did that just as soon as we opened her front door!

The thing I remember about this particular Thanksgiving get-together is that she had a picture in her kitchen of a beautiful meadow in a peaceful valley, and off in the distance was a majestic snow-covered mountain that rose very high above the clouds. I asked Gramma if that was a picture of near-by Mt. Rainier, and she said, "No, that's a picture of Life. See that mountain? There's a thousand paths to the top, but they all lead to the same place. It's not important which path you choose, but **choose one and keep climbing!**" Very wise advice!

During my lifetime, I have successfully climbed the career ladders as a Naval Officer, and as a Technical & Operational Satellite Communications Manager, and my linear, logical left-brain mind had always carried me through the challenges I faced. I had always learned what to do and what not to do to be a success, but the list of things I needed to do better kept getting longer and longer. However, it wasn't until I chose to opt out of the corporate structure and became an "energy healer" that I really came to appreciate Gramma's wisdom. I learned that the hand placements I had been taught in Reiki, the sweeping motions through a person's energy field I had learned in Healing Touch,

and a host of "you-must-do-it-this-way-for it-to-work" processes
in many additional energy techniques were simply training wheels
to let left-brain people begin to work in the right-brain world of
healing energies. Yet these training wheels can be very
beneficial, and in some cases necessary, for those who may be
new to that world. Those who are already effective remote energy
healers may find that they have moved beyond the technique-
structure of information in this book, but if there is a nugget or
two here, please feel free to incorporate them into your own
healing toolbox.

Purpose. The purpose of this book is to provide, for the person
who is ready to step into their mastery as an energy healer, a
collection of "training wheels" that I have found to be very useful
for reducing or eliminating a wide range of conditions that limit
the effectiveness of a healing session. This process that I call
"Trans-Scalar Healing" is a holistic remote healing technique
involving the application of healing Scalar Energies as well as
Angelic assistance to modify the human energy field in a way that
promotes a noticeable increase in physical, emotional, mental and
spiritual well-being, a state generally called "better health." In
this technique, we synthesize and integrate three primary healing
components – Scalar Energy, our entire personal energy field
(aura), and spiritual assistance – into a single, integrated process
that, once learned, can then be taught by anyone to anyone
anywhere.

Origin of "Trans-Scalar". In Physics, a "Scalar" quantity
describes a variable that has a numerically real magnitude, but no
direction of movement in our perceived Third-Dimensional reality
(for instance, speed, voltage or temperature). "Transcendent" is
defined by the Oxford Dictionary as "exceeding usual limits" or
"lying beyond or above the range of normal or merely physical
human experience." Trans-Scalar can therefore be thought of as
being "beyond the limits of Scalar Energy," and in this case, we
are also expanding the limits of human consciousness into the
realm of non-ordinary experiences.

Organization of the Book. The Trans-Scalar Healing (TSH) technique presented in this book introduces some concepts that may be new to the reader; therefore, the first three chapters discuss (1) what Scalar Energy is, how it can be created within your own energy field (aura), and its ability to restore greater health in living systems. It is not necessary to fully understand the details of this chapter, other than to recognize that Scalar Energy exists and can be focused and directed by the human mind to help clear and repair the energy field of another person; (2) the functions and characteristics of the three major components of the human energy field – the seven primary chakras associated with the physical body, the several primary energy meridians, and the five energy bodies of our being: the physical, etheric, emotional, mental and spiritual energy bodies; and (3) the spiritual realms of existence beyond our 3rd Dimensional physical reality. However, these first three chapters are provided only so the reader can, if desired, establish a knowledgeable foundation for understanding the actual healing procedures presented in Chapter 4.

Chapter 1 provides an overview of methods to generate Scalar energy within both the laboratory and a person's individual energy field (aura); in addition, it provides a comparison of the characteristics of Scalar energy and common forms of electromagnetic energy such as light, radio, electricity, etc. Also included is a discussion of Scalar energy's potential for use in healing the cells, tissues and organs of a living person's physical body. Again, the information in this chapter is provided for background purposes for the reader who wishes to understand what Scalar Energy is and its use in the Trans-Scalar Healing process.

Chapter 2 discusses the three primary elements of a human body's energetic composition in terms of its energy chakras, energy bodies and energy meridians; the functions of each of these energetic elements are described as they relate to and ultimately determine the overall state of health experienced by the individual. The physical body is composed of and surrounded by several inter-penetrating electromagnetic energy fields that are affected by the introduction of external energies; therefore, this Chapter provides an understanding of what is being affected in a positive manner when external healing energies such as Scalar Energy (or other traditional forms of healing energies such as Reiki, Healing Touch, Theta Healing, etc.) are applied with the intention of repatterning or restoring the recipient's energies. In addition to the discussion above, the end of the chapter contains information regarding "Permission for Healing".

Chapter 3 addresses the transcendent component of this unique healing technique by introducing the reader to several spiritual sources of information and healing energies within the higher dimensions of existence, a "place" that I just call my "Spiritual Area". The Healing Angels and Archangels are always ready to assist you in your Spiritual Area as the healing facilitator returns the client to the greatest level of health that his or her Higher Self, or soul, allows.

Chapter 4 provides detailed, step-by-step procedures for a complete remote Trans-Scalar Healing session where your client is not in your physical presence. The resulting Trans-Scalar Healing technique has proven to be very flexible; the general procedures described here can be used for addressing the physical, emotional, mental and spiritual needs of yourself and/or clients who may be anywhere on Earth. In addition, these procedures also bring higher-dimensional healing energies to Mother Earth.

Chapter 4 also provides the procedures that have been developed for documenting remote Trans-Scalar Healing sessions with human clients. However, these procedures are provided only as a guideline for exchanging information with your clients; please feel free to expand upon and modify or enhance these procedures as appropriate for your own situation and clientele.

While developing and refining the Trans-Scalar Healing processes, I have conducted both local healing sessions (the client was in my physical presence) and remote healing sessions (the client was not in my physical presence, and could be anywhere in the world). The healing results were equally apparent in either case; however, I soon chose to concentrate solely on remote healing, since working with a client in my physical presence audibly and visually distracted me from the expanded state of awareness I felt was necessary for close interaction with the spiritual assistance available. Therefore, the remote healing process described in this chapter may need to be appropriately modified for local healing sessions.

An additional benefit of working only remotely is that it ensures that the practitioner learns to trust their own intuitive ability to receive information from external sources, information that is personally relevant for their clients; further, this ability continues to be noticeably enhanced and reinforced with each remote spiritual healing session provided. As I have developed and practiced this technique, the only information I want to know about the client before the session is conducted is their full name and physical address at the time of the remote healing; this format of working "blind" to their physical, emotional and mental condition and symptoms requires me to rely solely on the information provided intuitively in my dialogues with my client's Higher Self and the Angelic assistants.

Chapter 5, the Afterword, provides a few examples of how the Trans-Scalar Healing process can help to accelerate the development of the practitioner's inner senses – particularly, his or her clairvoyant, clairaudient and clairsentient abilities.

<u>**Background.**</u> Trans-Scalar Healing (TSH) is an advanced remote spiritual/energetic healing technique that can be easily learned and practiced by anyone, regardless of whether or not they have been trained in any other energy healing technique such as Reiki, Healing Touch, Qi Gong, etc. TSH combines into a

single, unified process the significant aspects of several breathwork and visualization modalities, as well as several individual healing processes that have been channeled from spiritual sources. However, the key ingredient that makes Trans-Scalar Healing so effective is that all the practitioner's healing work is done while they are in an expanded dimension or state of consciousness (a state of awareness that I just call my "Spiritual Area") that allows the practitioner to consciously call on and interact directly with higher spiritual beings, including the Healing Angels, Ascended Masters, and Archangels.

There are several methods that have been successfully used to expand one's awareness into the higher dimensions of mind. One is to engage one's mind in deep and purposeful meditation, perhaps for several years, until an expanded or "enlightened" state of mind is reached; however, few people will have the patience and determination to achieve this state of awareness without a spiritual teacher or mentor to guide them along the way, and I am one of those people.

As an aside, one more efficient method is to place yourself into an expanded state of conscious awareness any time you wish through self-hypnosis. This has proven to be very effective, as documented in my 2015 book, **"Spiritual Journeys: A Practical Methodology for Accelerated Spiritual Development and Experiential Exploration;"** however, it requires that a skilled and trained Certified Hypnotist teach you the fundamentals of Self-Hypnosis so you can begin to use it on your own. To overcome this limitation, I developed the current Trans-Scalar Healing method of accessing an expanded state of consciousness without relying on self-hypnosis so that the complete healing technique can be used by anyone anywhere.

From 1995 to 1998, I had a unique opportunity to study several meditation and energy healing techniques taught by the many metaphysical practitioners in the Virginia Beach, VA area. After attending several "how-to-meditate" workshops without experiencing much success in reaching higher or expanded states of awareness, I found the one technique that worked for me: The Seven Terraces Meditation technique developed by the late Rev. Paul Solomon (www.paulsolomon.org). This technique didn't ask me to "quiet my body and empty my mind to the beauty and grandeur of the Universe." Instead, it kept my conscious mind actively involved by rapidly visualizing the narrative that provided fast-paced images and feelings involving all the physical senses with little time between the moving scenes to stop and think. Eventually, the meditation narrative moved me from an actively involved analytical perspective to a somatic or feeling experience of a neutral, non-analytic observer – from my linear thinking mind into my feeling heart – a vastly different way of experiencing my environment than what my former technical engineering background had taught me.

I added to Paul's Seven Terraces Meditation the additional information I had gained during the process, and renamed it the Inner Light Consciousness Meditation (ILC) technique. This process provided a wonderful guided visualization that led me through my physical world of sensory experiences into my energetic world that explored and balanced the energies in each of my seven primary chakras, and ultimately guided me into the spiritual world as I entered my own Inner Temple. As I explored my Inner Temple, I found the Healing Room with Archangel Raphael and the Healing Angels, the Hall of Records where I could "read" my own past lives as previous experiences in other bodies at other times, the Learning Room where I could ask my spiritual mentor (whom I "saw" as Merlin the Magician) any question at all, and the Meditation Room where I could explore anything, anywhere, any time.

Virginia Beach is a large vibrant community with all walks of metaphysicians and practitioners who offer not only meditation workshops and training, but also many alternative energy healing techniques; for a total of three years, I became a "workshop-a-holic" trained in Reiki, Healing Touch, Healing With Color &

Sound, Breathwork, RoHun, Reflective Healing, and several others. Subsequently, I trained in Reconnective Healing, Theta Healing, Healing Touch for Animals, and Bio-Scalar Healing; as a Certified Hypnotherapist, I am also trained and certified in Hypnotic Regression Therapy, Past Life Regression, Spiritual Regression, and Life Between Lives Therapy. Although this training was initially useful to me for understanding the models for energetic healing, as noted before, it is not necessary to already be proficient in any energy healing technique when learning and applying the processes and procedures of Trans-Scalar Healing.

Always curious about how things worked, I investigated several experiments dealing with several healing applications of Scalar Energy. In the early 1900's, Nikola Tesla noted that damaged living organisms could be returned to better health when placed in a Scalar Energy field. My own exploration of this application was spurred by Dr. Valerie Hunt's discovery and documentation that a Scalar Energy field can be generated within a person's aura using only intentional visualization and breathwork exercises with very effective and beneficial results on all levels of a person's being: physical, emotional, mental and spiritual.

With the steady, gentle inspiration from my Spirit Guide, once in my Spiritual Area, I could call on the Higher Self of my clients, challenge and verify the identity of all beings in my presence, and banish all deceivers and intruders. I could then safely move with my client's Higher Self to the Temple of Healing to work with the Angelic kingdom in a remarkably effective process adapted from ILC Meditation's Healing Room and also from the 'White Light Angels' healing technique developed by the Denver Hypnotherapist Greg McHugh, and to generate and provide higher dimensional Bio-Scalar healing energies for the benefit of my clients.

Later, additional spiritual guidance was received from my Spirit Guide and from Ascended Lady Master Kwan Yin to supplement this remarkable individual healing process with the Planetary Healing Process described herein. The resulting Trans-Scalar Healing technique has proven to be very flexible, in that the general procedures described here can be used for self-healing, as well as for addressing the physical, emotional, mental and spiritual needs of clients who can be anywhere in the world at all. In addition, TSH brings healing energies to Mother Earth (Gaia) and to the Collective Consciousness of Humanity, making it a wonderful holistic healing modality on all levels.

It should also be noted that, since everything in this and other universes is fundamentally comprised of energy, energy healing techniques can be applied to the energetic components and elements of the recipient of the energy, whether that recipient is alive (e.g., human, animal, plant, etc.), or energetic (e.g., causes, situations, relationships, etc.). However, the Trans-Scalar Healing processes described in this book are primarily intended for use with humans.

Comments or suggestions for improving the healing and communication process described would be appreciated; please discuss them with me at howard@howardbatie.com. Thank you.

Howard Batie
Chehalis, WA
September 2017

Chapter 1
Scalar Energy

What Is Scalar Energy? To understand Scalar Energy and its application within a healing technique, the following information may be useful. Scalar energy has always existed; however, only recently have scientists discovered how to measure it and make use of it. The possible existence of Scalar energy was first theorized in 1873 in a series of four groundbreaking equations by the Scottish mathematician, James Clerk Maxwell. [Endnote 1]. But it was several decades later when Nicola Tesla actually demonstrated the existence of Scalar energy. [Endnote 2] When Tesla died, he took the secrets of Scalar energy generation with him, and it took several decades before science was once again able to positively demonstrate the existence of Scalar energy in the laboratory and to explore its potential.

To better understand the nature of Scalar Energy, imagine a wave of energy, such as a radio signal, a beam of light, or a wave on the surface of the ocean, traveling from left to right at a steady frequency and a steady amplitude toward the point in space labeled "A", as shown in Figure 1a, and another wave of energy flowing from right to left toward point A at exactly the same frequency and amplitude as the first wave. At that one point in space, both waves are in precisely the same phase; that is, the amplitudes of both waves rise and fall in unison with each other at point A. The result is a condition that Newtonian Physics describes as "Constructive Interference" where the resultant effect, at that at point A, one could observe and measure a resulting wave of energy of the original frequency, but it would have an amplitude ("height") of twice that of either original wave (ignoring the effects of friction), as shown in Fig. 1b.

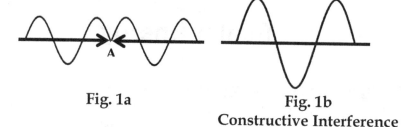

Fig. 1a   **Fig. 1b**

Constructive Interference

Referring to Figure 2a, now consider the original wave of energy still flowing from left to right at a steady frequency and amplitude, and at point B it encounters another wave of exactly the same frequency and amplitude coming from exactly the opposite direction, but 180 degrees completely out of phase with the first wave. At point A where the two waves meet, the first wave's amplitude will be rising as it passes through that point, but the second wave's amplitude will be falling exactly an **equal** and **opposite** amount. The result is called "Destructive Interference" since at point B, it <u>appears</u> that there is no energy at all – the radio signal fades completely, the light seems to go out, and no waves appear at all on the surface of the water.

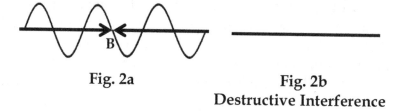

Fig. 2a   **Fig. 2b**

Destructive Interference

However, there is a lot of energy coming into Point B from each of the waves. So, what happened to that energy? There is a fundamental principle in Physics that says that energy can neither be created nor destroyed – it can only change its form. Therefore, in this case, it appears that the energy we would normally be able to detect and measure in the physical world has now been transformed into something that cannot be registered with our physical eyes or instruments. At Point B, it <u>appears</u> as if the energy of both waves has been transformed into another "non-physical" form of energy that cannot be measured with our current physical instruments, and we call that form "Scalar Energy".

Comparison of Scalar and Electromagnetic Energy.

Scalar energy differs from traditional electromagnetic energy in several significant ways, as shown in Table 1. First, Scalar Energy has no frequency associated it. Physicists refer to it as Non-Hertzian Energy because frequency is measured in Hertz, or cycles per second, and Scalar Energy has no frequency of operation. Secondly, Scalar Energy does not propagate like normal electricity or light does. Most Electromagnetic Energy propagates at or near the speed of light, depending on the medium through which it travels; however, Scalar Energy appears to demonstrate the quantum characteristics of immediately being everywhere.

Normal Electromagnetic Energy also decreases in strength the farther you get from the source – the radio station, or from the shining light, for example; but Scalar Energy is very different – its strength is not affected by either distance or time. These features of Scalar Energy should provide a tantalizing clue as to the real nature of Scalar Energy, since Scalar Energy can only be adequately described by the higher mathematics of Quantum Physics.

Energy Comparison	
Electro-Magnetic	**Scalar Energy**
Radio, Electricity, Light Always Has Frequency	No Waves, Therefore, No Frequency
Field of Movement	Static "Standing" Field
Propagates Thru Medium	Is Located Everywhere
Strength Decreases With Distance	Strength Not Affected By Distance Or Time
Described By Newtonian Physics, Mechanics	Described By Quantum Physics, Mechanics

Table I. Energy Comparison

Generation Of Scalar Energy In The Laboratory. One
way scientists have been able to generate Scalar Energy in the
laboratory is to use a special configuration of winding for coils.
In Figure 3a, passing an electric current through a standard coil of
wire generates both an electric field and a magnetic field, called
the EM field, in the space around the coil, as shown by the dashed
lines of the EM field. But if you have a bifilar coil, or double
coil, as shown in Figure 3b and pass an electric current in one
direction through one winding of the coil and an identical electric
current of exactly the same frequency and amplitude and phase,
but flowing in the opposite direction in the second winding of the
coil, the directional vector components of their external electric
and magnetic fields cancel each other completely, creating a
Scalar (non-physical) Energy field that cannot be measured with
our standard physical instruments. We can, however, be sure that
a field of energy has been generated by noticing and measuring its
effects on physical objects, including living tissues and
organisms.

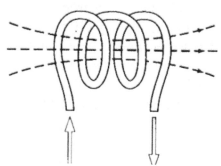

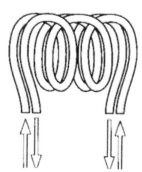

Fig. 3a. Standard Coil   Fig. 3b. Bifilar Coil

Effects of Scalar Energy on Living Tissues. Biophysicist
and cell biologist Dr. James Oschman, Ph.D., is one of the few
academic scientists who has conducted extensive research
regarding the effects of electromagnetic and Scalar waves on
living organisms. [Endnote 3] He has illustrated how Scalar
waves can be generated by passing an electric current through a
bifilar-wound coil or a singly-wound coil around a moibus-shaped

ferro-magnetic core. The Scalar field is developed when the magnetic and electric components of a waveform cancel each other. Although we do not as yet have instruments that can reliably measure the absolute intensity or magnitude of the Scalar energy, we can reliably infer that a Scalar energy field has been generated by monitoring and recording the effects of this energy and its Scalar field on living matter such as seeds and human and animal tissues. The Scalar field has properties that are quite different from those of a conventional electromagnetic field such as that generated by a radio or TV station or the microwave in your kitchen.

A team of Japanese scientists has documented that the average biomagnetic strength of a normal energy healer's palm chakra has been measured with a reading of approximately 1 microgauss on a sensitive magnetometer. But when the same trained healer focused on healing, the biomagnetic strength rose to approximately 1 milligauss, 1000 times stronger [Endnote 4], a feat that the average untrained person was unable to demonstrate [Endnote 5]. The implications regarding the intentions of the mind should be quite apparent.

Dr. Zimmerman of the University of Colorado School of Medicine noted that the biomagnetic field strength emanating from the healer's hands was not constant, but varied regularly within a specific range of frequencies. He reported that the frequency of variation in the field strength of the healer's hand chakra biomagnetic field slowly varied from approximately 0.3 cycles per second (cps) up to about 30 cps, and then back down again to about 0.3 cps, and this pattern continued to repeat as long as the healer intended to "send" healing energies to someone. Further investigations reported by Sisken & Walker [Endnote 6] found that at 2 cps, damaged nerves were either repaired or regenerated; at 7 cps, bones knitted together very rapidly; at 10 cps, ligaments and soft muscle tissue healed very rapidly; and at 15 cps capillary formation, fibroblast proliferation and decreased skin necrosis were demonstrated.

However, in contrast to many frequencies that the normal electromagnetic Human Energy Field responds to, a Scalar field has no fundamental frequency. Instead of running along wires or radiating out like radio waves, Scalar energy instead does not propagate through space, as do electromagnetic frequencies, but instead remains static in the area where it was created. Scalar energy is also an energy that can be charged or "informed" with additional energetic information, much like a radio station's fundamental broadcast frequency (e.g., 1000 Kilocycles per second) is modulated by the information of the program being broadcast (e.g., music or vocal information). And most importantly for our discussion here, the focused intentions used in Scalar energy healings has demonstrated profoundly beneficial effects on living matter – not only on living tissue and organs, but even on human DNA. [Endnote7] Preliminary experimental laboratory results of Dr. Glen Rein show that "...quantum fields produce larger biological responses than classical EM (electro-magnetic) fields.... (and that) these quantum fields have unusual properties, e.g. non-local action at a distance." [Endnote 8]

Generation of Scalar Energy Within The Human Body. Dr. Oschman has illustrated how Scalar waves can be generated in the laboratory; however, parallel research has also been conducted to determine if Scalar wave energy can be self-generated within the human body, and if so, how. The late Dr. Valerie V. Hunt, Professor Emeritus of Physiological Sciences at the University of California at Los Angeles, was a world-renowned research scientist and authority on the human generation of Scalar energies, and she coined the term "Bio-Scalar" to refer to the ability to generate Scalar energy within the human body and energy field. This ability is evidently apparent in everyone, not just trained energy healers. On her professional website (www.valerievhunt.com), she states,

> "Recently another form of electromagnetism that is organized into a different pattern has been discovered. It is no longer a wave but is changed to a standing or stationary

energy. In physics, this is called a Scalar wave. When it exists inside the body, it is called a bio-Scalar wave. This Scalar energy does not flow like waves, but it does occupy space and increases in spatial mass. The energy that we experience in our bodies is electromagnetic waves radiating from the atoms of all our tissue cells. ... If such electro-magnetic waves meet head on at 180 degrees (out of phase) with another wave of the same frequency, a Scalar wave is created. This means that the energy from the two like waves does not take another direction or even a different frequency. Instead, it becomes an enfolded or standing Scalar field. At first this Scalar energy was believed to be a vacuum. Now it is known that it is a dynamic pile of non-directional energy." [Endnote 9]

Dr. Hunt further states that, "When the mind field is consciously focused, intent can direct electromagnetic frequencies to enter the body from opposite ends of a straight ... line from front to back, from up to down, from right to left, placing bio-Scalar energy in the trunk, head and legs." [Endnote 10] Using a particular sequence of specific breathing exercises and intentional visualizations, she has developed a technique that is designed to generate a Scalar energy field within the human body. These exercises essentially ask the student to use their mind to imagine or visualize the electro-magnetic frequencies of our known three-dimensional universe collapsing in a specific sequence and manner into an infinitesimal point of Scalar energy within us and then, again through intention, to direct the Scalar field to expand to encompass our entire human energy field. [Endnote 11] This has proven itself to be a very useful and effective process, especially when moving our awareness beyond the limitations of our physical body and into a higher state of expanded consciousness and awareness, into a higher "dimension" of our being. In this higher vibrational frequency, we can, through intention, expand and direct this Bio-Scalar field not only for our own highest and best good, but also for that of others as well.

Although Dr. Hunt's process has provided the foundational ability to self-generate a field of healing Bio-Scalar energy, further experimentation has led to development of additional techniques that transcend the effectiveness of Bio-Scalar energy alone. This is accomplished by intentionally focusing the application of self-generated Scalar energy while also enlisting the aid and assistance of the Angelic Kingdom.

From the above discussion, we know that Scalar Energy exists and that we are expanding our understanding of its beneficial effects on living tissues and organisms. Because we also recognize that Scalar Energy is a quantum form of energy, it can be intentionally focused and directed by human consciousness with the purpose of modifying or repatterning the energy field of another human. The next chapter discusses the energetic elements of the composite human energy field, which are the objective or target of our focused intentions during a Trans-Scalar Healing session.

Chapter 2
The Human Energy Field & Healing

The human energy field responds to
stimuli even before the brain does. I think
we have way overrated the brain as the
active ingredient in the relationship of a
human to the world. The mind's not in the
brain. It's in that darn field!

Dr. Valerie Hunt, quoted by Michael Talbot
in *The Holographic Universe*

As astronomers gaze farther and deeper into the heavens, they
continue to come across processes in other galaxies and other
worlds for which they have no explanation. Clearly, our present
understanding of the composition of the universe is less than
perfect. In an attempt to correct this situation, astronomers and
astrophysicists have begun to re-examine some of their basic
theories and concepts of nature. The Newtonian concept of our
physical world worked very well when we were not aware of the
vast fields of energy that permeate all levels of the universe, from
the largest galaxies to the smallest atom.

The Universal Energy Field (UEF)
There appears to be a source of energy within our universe that is,
as yet, unexplained by modern science. However, more than one
physicist has speculated that our universe began its existence as a
subtle energy field of very high vibrational frequencies that cannot
normally be physically felt or observed, and in some places this
field gradually became denser and denser over time, with
subsequently lower vibrational patterns. Eventually, these areas of
denser vibrational patterns coalesced into what we now perceive as
our physical universe of galaxies, stars and planets. It is also
speculated that, in the immensity of space within our universe, the

energy field from which all matter coalesced is still there. This original energy field is of a higher vibratory rate than our physical third-dimensional world, and is theorized to contain the holographic pattern for all of physical creation. This vast sea of vibrational energy is beyond the reach of today's instruments, and is termed the Universal Energy Field, or UEF.

In her groundbreaking book on energy-based healing, *Hands of Light* [Endnote 1], Barbara Brennan lists several potential characteristics of the UEF. According to her, the UEF is probably composed of a type of energy previously undefined by western science, and which may exist in a state between what we consider matter and energy. Furthermore, she speculates that this energy permeates all animate and inanimate objects in the universe, as well as connects all objects with each other. It cannot be perceived or sensed by our physical senses of touch, taste, smell, sight and sound, but can only be experienced through the perception of our higher or inner senses, what she calls our Higher Sense Perception. And lastly, she suggests that this energy is creative in that it is consistently building form, as opposed to degenerating form; i.e., it is synergistic instead of entropic. If Brennan's observations are accurate, we are indeed becoming aware of our universe as much, much more than we can see and measure with today's instruments.

The Human Energy Field (HEF)

The Human Energy Field (HEF) is "...that part of the UEF associated with the human body" [Endnote 2], and can be described from three different perspectives: in terms of (1) the major and minor chakras throughout the body, (2) the subtle energy fields or energy bodies which surround the physical body, and (3) the energy meridians within the physical body which provide the means of circulating and distributing energy (e.g., prana, chi, ki, etc.) to the tissues and organs of the body. Each of these perspectives is discussed below.

The Chakra System. The Sanskrit word "chakra" means literally "spinning wheel". To those who can clairvoyantly see energy fields, each of the seven major chakras resembles a spinning wheel when looking directly into the chakra. However, when viewed from the side, it looks more like an energy vortex somewhat resembling the shape of a tornado or a funnel. This energy funnel is tight and compact near the surface of the skin, and gradually widens as it extends outside the physical body to the outer edge of the aura.

The chakra system within the human body consists of seven major chakras and many minor chakras. The location of the seven major chakras is shown in Figure 4. Each major chakra from the Root through Brow Chakra has four energy vortices associated with it: one spiraling upward, one downward toward the earth, one out the front of the physical body, and one out through the back of the body. The upward projecting vortex from one chakra, and the downward projecting vortex of the chakra just above it, join together to form an energy column that runs vertically through the physical body from the bottom of the spine (Root Chakra) up in front of the spine and out through the top of the head (Crown Chakra). The Crown Chakra also has four vortices oriented the same as the lower six chakras; however, the vortices of the Crown Chakra are spatially so close to the vortices of the Brow Chakra that they overlap and are often confused. Nevertheless, the energies of the Crown and Brow Chakras can be separately identified by their individual frequencies.

When a major chakra is "healthy and balanced" its front and rear vortices spin in a circular motion. However, if there is a disturbance or blockage in the flow of energy within a chakra, the circular motion may become elliptical or, in extreme cases, severely flattened on its sides. This distortion may be sensed by those able to see or feel energy fields, or indirectly sensed by a pendulum. Further, each chakra has its own specific "frequency" or rate of spin, with the lowest rate of spin in the Root Chakra, and steadily increasing up to the highest rate of spin in the Crown Chakra.

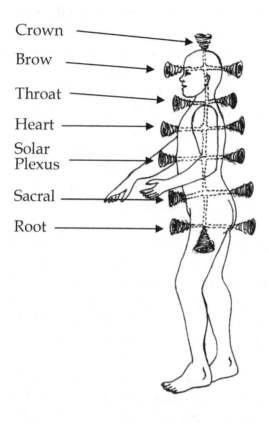

Crown

Brow

Throat

Heart

Solar
Plexus

Sacral

Root

Figure 4. The Human Chakra System

Function Of The Chakra System. The purpose or
function of the human chakra system is to take in specific
frequencies of higher-dimensional energy from the Universal
Energy Field all around us and translate or step down its frequency
of vibration to that which can be used within the physical body.
Each major chakra vibrates or spins at a different rate, and each
chakra will absorb energy from the UEF that is harmonically related
to its own frequency. Thus, energy from several frequency bands
within the infinitely broad UEF spectrum is absorbed by the
different chakras and is directed to those organs with which each
chakra is associated (see Table II). A good analogy of how this
occurs is to visualize all the many TV signals existing around us

Table II. Major Chakras and Associated Organs and Glands.

Chakra	Associated Organs	Endocrine Gland
Crown	Upper Brain, Right Eye	Pineal
Brow	Ears, Nose, Lower Brain, Nervous System, Left Eye	Pituitary
Throat	Lungs, Larynx, Alimentary Canal	Thyroid, Parathyroid
Heart	Heart, Blood, Vagus Nerve, Circulatory System	Thymus
Solar Plexus	Stomach, Gall Bladder, Liver	Pancreas
Sacral	Reproductive System	Testes, Ovaries
Root	Spinal Column, Kidneys	Adrenals

all the time; by tuning to a specific channel (frequency), we get the specific information or programming being sent on that frequency. The human chakra system can then be said to act as a sort of multichannel receiver of vibrational frequencies from different portions of the energy spectrum all around us.

Through the internal human energy distribution system (see "Meridians" below), each chakra is also connected to specific organs and endocrine glands, as shown in Table II. For instance, the particular energy vibrations or frequencies absorbed by the Solar Plexus Chakra are linked energetically to the stomach, pancreas, gall bladder and liver. Likewise, the reproductive organs receive their components of energy from the UEF through the Sacral Chakra.

Many minor chakras are also located throughout the body, and are usually associated with joints such as the knee, shoulder, elbow, etc. Additional secondary chakras are found in the palms of both hands and the soles of the feet. These minor chakras appear as beams of energy emanating from the body rather than the spinning vortices of the major chakras. At least two major healing modalities (Reiki and Healing Touch) take advantage of these beams of energy coming out of the center of the palms and from the fingertips to stimulate and accelerate the body's own healing processes.

Importance Of "Clearing" The Chakras. Advanced practitioners of several energy healing techniques have noted a strong correlation of strong emotional energies (e.g., unworthiness, fear, anxiety, etc.) and specific chakras, as reflected in Table III. The faulty thoughts and limiting beliefs that cause these distorted emotional reactions must be removed through some energetic process in order to return the chakra to full functioning of its intended purpose. The easiest and quickest way to do this is through a powerful visualization process that "spins" colored energy associated with each chakra into it in a circular (non-distorted) fashion, setting up the correct frequency-specific energy field that can entrain other energies to the correct vibration in that region, thus "balancing" or "clearing" the distorted energies. For the remaining stubborn emotional issues that are not responsive to purely energetic repatterning, the assistance of a Certified Hypnotist or Hypnotherapist trained in Regression Therapies is suggested.

Table III. Chakras And Typical Faulty Thoughts.

Chakra	Color	General Issue	Typical Faulty Thought
Root	Red	How I See Myself	I'm not worthy of abundance.
Sacral	Orange	How I Feel About Myself	I'm afraid of making a mistake.
Solar Plexus	Yellow	How I Think About Myself	I'm not in control of my life.
Heart	Green	How I Care About Myself	If I love, I'll be hurt.
Throat	Blue	How I Express Myself	If I speak out, I'll be ridiculed.
Brow	Indigo	How I Perceive Myself	I must always be perfect.
Crown	Violet	How I Feel My Purpose	Life is an exercise in futility.

Energy Bodies. The Human Energy Field, or aura, is made up of a number of individual but harmonically related energetic bodies, each vibrating at its own frequency. All these subtle energy bodies are actually spatially superimposed within and around the physical form, which is also an energy body that vibrates at the lower frequencies which are within the range of our physical eyes. Above the vibrational energy of the physical body are the higher 'octaves' of the Etheric Body, the Emotional Body, the Mental Body, and the Spiritual Body [Endnote 4]. Each energy body surrounds and interpenetrates all lower energy bodies, including the physical body. For example, the Mental Energy Body surrounds and penetrates the Emotional, Etheric and Physical Bodies. The human energy bodies are depicted in Figure 5.

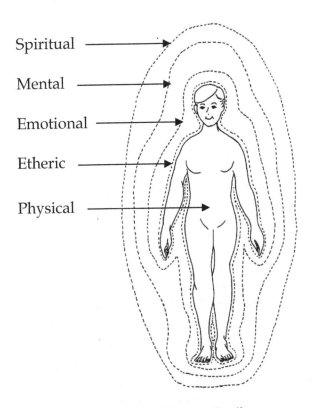

Spiritual

Mental

Emotional

Etheric

Physical

Figure 5. Human Energy Bodies

If it is difficult to visualize the superimposed and interpenetrating energy bodies of our Human Energy Field, think of the many radio and TV signals that are penetrating your body and existing simultaneously within the same space as your body. Moving through all "solid" matter is a constant barrage of vibrations which is far above our ability to detect with our physical senses. Tune in to the right frequency with the proper receiver, and you can listen to your favorite radio station; tune in to even higher frequencies and you get the evening news on Channel 7. Above these frequencies are heat, light, ultraviolet radiation, x-rays and highly energetic particles of cosmic radiation. All these vibrations exist simultaneously within the same three-dimensional space that our body occupies, and the only characteristic that differentiates one energy from another is frequency, the rate at which that particular "kind" of energy vibrates.

The Physical Energy Body. At first, it may seem unusual to consider that the physical body is an energy body, but that is exactly what it appears to be. The physical body is the densest form of energy that our consciousness uses to explore and interact with its environment. Think about that for a moment. By the densest form, I mean that the vibrational patterns of the physical body are of a frequency low enough to be seen by our eyes (they are within the spectrum of visible light), heard by our ears (about 30 to 15,000 Hertz), and experienced with the senses of touch, taste and smell which are within the "frequency capability" of our physical sense organs.

Our physical body is really a composite field of energy frequencies that have coalesced from the higher, less dense octaves. And we also need to remember that as vibrating fields interact with each other, one field can affect another field through the phenomenon of sympathetic vibration and resonance. If a violin player produces a note an octave above Middle C, and a second violin lying nearby on a table has a string which is tuned to Middle C, the second violin string tuned to Middle C will sympathetically begin to vibrate as well. So, as we also begin to understand that there are several vibrational fields of energy around our physical body, it becomes easier to understand how one field affects another through this principle. And this is the key to understanding how energy-based healing techniques can achieve such visible and profound results in the physical energy body.

The Etheric Energy Body. The etheric body is the first energy body an "octave" in frequency above the frequencies of the physical body. It exists within the physical body, and extends outward about an inch or two outside the skin of the physical body. Its purpose is to provide an energy template or energy pattern for the development, maintenance and repair of the physical body. The etheric body contains a vibrational energy counterpart for each organ, blood vessel and bone found in the physical body. Indeed, the etheric body contains the energetic blueprint for the pathways that guide the location and development of every cell of the physical body. "The bony structure, muscular, and vascular tissues, the nerves, the brain, and other substances are all represented in the etheric mold by currents of energy on specific frequencies." [Endnote 5] "The physical tissues exist as such only because of the vital (etheric) field behind them; that it, the (etheric) field is prior to, not a result of, the physical body." [Endnote 6]

Since the etheric body is the physical body's blueprint, the two are very closely related. The energetic vibrations of the etheric body determine the pattern for not only the physical tissues and organs, but also the state of health of those tissues and organs. If the vibrations are not clear and pure, this disharmony will be reflected in the physical body as disharmonious functions -- what we call "disease". Conversely, traumas to the physical body (e.g., broken bones, burns, incisions and scars) will in time be reflected into the etheric body unless there is some interceding process that either prevents this reflection into the etheric body or which restores the original vibrational pattern which existed prior to the trauma. The ability to work with a client's vibrating energy fields is precisely what forms the basis for rapid and effective energy-based physical healings.

As explained by Talbot, an illness can appear in the energy field weeks and even months before it appears in the physical body. He considers that the physical body "...is just one more level of density in the human energy field and is itself a kind of hologram that has coalesced out of the interference patterns of the aura...." [Endnote 7]

The following description of the etheric and higher subtle energy bodies surrounding the physical body are taken from Barbara Brennan's book, *Hands of Light*. The etheric body appears as a grid of tiny energy lines which has the overall structure and shape of the physical body. It is upon this etheric grid or matrix that the cells and tissues of the body develop and are anchored. The etheric body appears as a light blue or gray matrix of lines of light that constantly pulsate or scintillate at a rate of from 15-20 cycles per minute.

The Emotional Energy Body. The next "octave" above the frequencies of the Etheric energy body is the Emotional energy body that contains the emotional patterns, feelings, and vibrations that determine how we feel about ourselves and interact with others. The emotional patterns, feelings, and vibrations within the Emotional energy body are our subconscious reactions to the beliefs about ourselves and others that are held in the Mental Energy Body. If we are constantly angry, always feel helpless, or are consistently fearful, these patterns or vibrations get locked in our emotional energy body and become a part of our personality. This determines to a very large degree how we interact with others on personal, social, and cultural levels.

The Mental Energy Body. The mental body contains the structure and patterns of all the thoughts and belief systems that we consider as true, and there is a very strong connection between the mental and emotional bodies. Although a thought or idea can in itself be very powerful, our reactions to those thoughts carry even more energy, and different people will react differently to the same thought or belief. For example, consider the thought form, "Men are better than women." One person might hear that thought or idea, think it was silly, and give it absolutely no energy. But another person might become very passionate, depending on their gender or greater belief systems, and argue strongly either for or against the truth of that statement. The emotional energy body would then record the intensity of the <u>reaction</u> to the thought or belief considered as true and stored in the mental energy body. However, the person who thought the statement was silly in the first place would not have any resonance with it, and no energetic pattern would be stored in either the mental or emotional energy bodies.

The Spiritual Energy Body. The spiritual body (i.e., all vibrational patterns in "octaves" higher than the mental energy body) contains all the information related to our experiences, and reflects our gestalt consciousness of all that has been learned and experienced throughout our soul's existence. It contains our higher intentions, our sense of what is right and wrong ("conscience"), the information and knowledge of all previous experiences, and our desires to increase our awareness of our purpose, place and mission for this lifetime.

These five energy bodies make up one's Human Energy Field, or aura. Its outer shape appears roughly egg-shaped and extends out to perhaps 1½ to two feet beyond the physical body; however, this shape can be extended even further out or contracted closer to the physical body, depending on the situation the person is experiencing. For example, when a person is feeling emotions of unconditional love, the aura may expand to several feet and radiate bright hues of gold or white; but if the same person is feeling threatened physically or emotionally, the entire aura may collapse for protection into a much denser pattern within only a few inches of the body.

Another key concept to be understood in this discussion of the five concentric energy fields that comprise each human is *that each field affects the one below it, but not the one above it.* For example, referring to Figure 5 above, the energetic thoughts and belief patterns held in the Mental energy body affect and determine the reactions and feelings held in the Emotional energy body. These emotional energy patterns such as anger, fear, unworthiness, guilt, etc., all affect the next lower energy body, the Etheric energy body which is the energetic pattern of template upon which our physical structure is built. As old cells die and are replaced by newly created cells, the Etheric energy patterns provide the blueprint for the new cells, thus ensuring that new stomach cells replace only the old stomach cells that die off. As stated in his book, *Vibrational Medicine*, Dr. Richard Gerber, MD writes, "The etheric body is a holographic energy template that guides the growth and development of the physical body." [Endnote 8] Much of the success of the Trans-Scalar Healing technique is because the negative or limiting thoughts and beliefs we hold about ourselves and others are addressed and repatterned, thus allowing the healing Scalar (or other) energy to remove the original cause (distorted beliefs and thoughts about self) of much of our negative emotional and physical conditions.

Energy Meridians. Within the body many energetic pathways connect each organ and chakra, both major and minor. It is this internal energy distribution system that permits the flow of life-sustaining energy to the internal organs and tissues. This system of pathways has been known and used for several thousand years by oriental practitioners of Acupuncture. In Acupuncture, the thought is that many diseases are caused or exacerbated by inadequate energy flow to certain areas of the body or organs. The fine needles used in Acupuncture stimulate specific points on these energy meridians to release the blocked flow of life-force energy, and thus restore a better state of health. More recently, a variation of this practice, Acupressure, has become quite popular. With Acupressure, stimulation of the energy meridians to release the blocked flow of energy is accomplished by applying physical pressure from the fingers or hands instead of Acupuncture needles. A further refinement of working with energy Meridians is the Emotional Freedom Technique (EFT), where an entire meridian can be cleared of energetic blockages by tapping only on the end points of the meridian.

When healing energy is transferred to the client's body through whatever means (such as the healer placing his hands on the client in a Reiki session), the energy meridians within the body provide the means of distributing the energy received from the healer to wherever it is needed within the body.

Permission For Healing

Many energy healers say we need the other person's permission or, if the client is a minor, their guardian's permission, to provide an energy healing. Furthermore, if the healing session is not a success, the healer is somehow to blame. I believe these concepts are short-sighted.

First, when you pray for someone, do you ask their permission first? No! I'm not aware of any religion or belief system in the world that says you need to have someone's permission before you pray for their health, their fortune, their safety, their welfare, or whatever you think the person wants. Dr. Eric Pearl, in *The Reconnection*, says, "You can only *offer* a healing; you can't *inflict* a healing." [Endnote 9] Simply stated, you, as the practitioner, are not in charge of whether or not your client responds positively to the healing energies offered. In Trans-Scalar Healing, we should not be concerned with what the client's conscious mind wants. Instead, our efforts should be simply to offer healing energies to the client, with the understanding that these energies will be accepted and incorporated by the client's Higher Self only if a healing is in the highest good of the client.

However, being unattached to the outcome has always been a challenge for me because I want people to feel better; I want them to get the healing they came for; I want them to be pain-free; I want to help others. In other words, I may become personally invested in the success of the healing session. But I'm not consciously aware of what is in their highest and best good from a spiritual or soul perspective; I don't consciously know what their soul has chosen to learn or experience in this incarnation. So instead, I invest myself in the healing *process*, but not in the *outcome*. I consciously focus my intention and all the healing energies I can muster up for the greatest possible healing that is appropriate for them at that time. This is stepping into my own Mastery and consciously acknowledging that each of us is a Co-Creator with the Angelic Realm and Spiritual Physicians to assist in co-creating the highest possible and most appropriate state of health for my clients at that time.

There are many energy healing modalities or techniques for spiritual healing, and some involve the participation of the Angelic Kingdom – the Healing Angels and/or Archangels. In many instances, the client's wellbeing is "turned over" to the Angels, who are asked to perform the healing techniques, because the practitioner cannot deliver them or feels uncomfortable or unworthy in that role. However, Trans-Scalar Healing stands out from other techniques in that the <u>practitioner</u> becomes the primary healing agent and performs the energetic healing processes himself or herself, with the Angels only providing support as directed by the practitioner.

Chapter 3
The Spiritual Realms

Not only is the universe grander than we imagine,
it's grander than we CAN imagine.

- J.B.S. Haldane (paraphrased)

The world that we think we live in is limited to what we are aware of – to what we can see, hear, touch, taste and smell; however, the world we actually exist in is not limited to what can be detected by the five senses of our physical bodies. In the physical domain, there are many energies and vibrations that are beyond the range of our sensory organs, such as the infra-red frequencies and the ultra-violet frequencies below and above the visible spectrum, respectively. There are also the infra-sonic frequencies of sound used by elephants to communicate, and the ultra-sonic frequencies of some birds and dolphins to communicate with others of their species.

In addition, the domain of existence above that of physical human beings is usually called the spiritual domain. In this context "spiritual" does not mean "religious;" instead, it is where many non-physical beings exist and, instead of communicating with physical light, sound and touch, use a much 'higher' spiritual means of communication to interact, such as telepathic exchange of entire packages of information containing all the visual imagery and complete emotional energy of their experiences, as well as the experiences of others. This is the "Spiritual Area" where intuitive clairvoyant, clairaudient, and clairsentient (simply 'knowing') information is exchanged during a Trans-Scalar Healing session.

Most people would say that we live in the Third Dimension of space where there is length, width and height of all objects that we can touch and interact with; however, this concept severely limits what is actually "real". What about the things that do not have physical length, depth or breadth? Is not an idea "real"? Is not a feeling "real"? I like to define my "reality" as being composed of anything that can affect me in any way, so some ideas are real to me and others are not. The belief that "My cat likes me because she purrs" is repeatedly reinforced as true through many separate interactions with her, but the belief that "The world is flat" does not resonate with me; so, to me, that belief is not real or true for me, and I give it no energy.

Dimensions of Physical Existence. In our daily experiences, we are constantly analyzing and making judgements about whether something is good or bad, safe or dangerous. Another perspective of how we live our life can be appreciated by observing the judgements we place on words, actions and feelings. For instance, we quickly learn that how we feel about ourselves is often determined by our intentions and interaction with others.

We humans have also been taught the concept that those 'higher' dimensions or areas of existence are 'above' us in the sense that we may believe 'Heaven' or 'Valhalla' or the 'Great Hunting Ground' is 'up in the sky' somewhere above us, but we are separated from this area because we believe we are somehow 'less' than the perfect beings in the sky. However, I prefer to believe that my Spiritual Area is an *Expanded State of Consciousness* right here on Earth. Instead of physically rising up higher into some enlightened space above us, we simply need to expand our awareness and become consciously aware of the spiritual dimensions that have always been right here with us all the time. Whether we see that or feel that, when we experience this expanded state of consciousness, we can begin interacting with it and communicating with its inhabitants. We figuratively 'ascend' in frequency, energy and ability as we develop and expand our state of consciousness. The "Ascension' is not physically rising into the clouds; instead it is the much more powerful and effective process of individually learning to use the higher frequency energies and abilities of the spiritual realms in our everyday physical lifetime – 'bringing heaven to earth'!

To develop the ability to access these higher dimensions of consciousness, it has been said that individuals must clear or release more than half (51% or greater) of their negative frequency patterns and attune themselves to at least a portion of the lower sub-level frequencies of the Fifth Dimension (see discussion below) in order to recall and begin using a portion of their innate spiritual abilities, such as using telepathy to communicate instead of using voice language. Therefore, a 'visit' to their Spiritual Area requires that one at least temporarily releases those energies and feelings that would interfere with accessing the Spiritual Area.

Ascension Of Human Consciousness. Channeled through Ronna Herman, Archangel Michael has provided a clear and understandable discussion of the first five Dimensions of the true reality in which we all exist; [Endnote 1] that discussion is provided below with permission. Each Dimension has seven sub-levels of gradually increasing expression of feelings, emotions and/or beliefs, and each of the five Dimensions is also gradually increasing in frequency and positive expression; there is no absolute dividing line between one sub-level and the next, or between one Dimension and the next.

First Dimension – The Mineral Kingdom. The First-Dimensional environment is the world of the elements, the building blocks of the material world from the sub-atomic elements to the soil, rocks and water that make up the body of the Earth. This is the foundation for the manifestation of all plant life, and home of the lowest level of the Elemental Kingdom whose mission is to relay from the sun the life-giving elements or nourishment for all of the mineral and plant kingdoms. Under the guidance of the Elemental Kingdom, the Plant Kingdom also began to experience an instinctual desire to reach for the sunlight and bask in the warmth of its radiance.

Second Dimension – The Plant and Animal Kingdoms.
The mid-Second-Dimensional level is where the Animal
Kingdom materialized and a sub-level of consciousness began.
Originally, the Animal Kingdom subsisted and received
sustenance from plant life, and it was never intended that they
should become carnivorous. Basic feelings and emotions began
to be displayed within the Second-Dimensional environment as
the Animal Kingdom evolved and began to experience primal
fear, anger and instinctual love or compatibility with a strong
desire for companionship. The Animal Kingdom is strongly
influenced by inborn instinct. The animals' Sparks come from
and return to a Group Soul in between each physical lifetime.

Third Dimension (First Three Sub-Planes) –
Animal/Nature Kingdom. These levels are home to the animals
who are gradually evolving into a higher species, and who have
developed a limited sentient intelligence, and are within this range
of intelligence, such as Primates (Apes and Monkeys), Elephants,
Horses, Dogs and Cats. In some future stage of the "Ascension
process," they may be ensouled and will be allotted an
individualized I AM consciousness.

There are also some humans whose first incarnational experiences
have been in this solar system or on the Earth Plane, and they are,
therefore, still functioning within an animal/human base-
instinctual nature, along with a varying degree of intellectual
capacity. However, there are no longer any young or early Souls
incarnating on the Earth Plane. Only mature and old Souls who
have had a vast number of incarnational experiences throughout
this Universe are incarnating on Earth now.

Third Dimension (Sub-Planes Four Through Seven) –
Human Kingdom. The Third-Dimensional realm of material
expression is more mentally focused, with a strong desire to
create, conquer and to control nature. It is the lowest level of
humankind's experiential existence. A basic, instinctual-survival

nature began to develop with a gradual, limited consciousness of self, *"I am separate and different from you."* Human Beings began to emerge from a herd-state of consciousness where there were seldom any unique or individualized thoughts. Most knowledge came forth from the group instinctual nature and basic concepts handed down from the elders.

Prevailing negative attributes to be overcome or released before ascending in consciousness from the Third to the Fourth Dimension include: survival instinct, fear, anger, vengefulness, hate, shame, guilt, denial, uncaring, apathetic, stubborn, miserable, indifferent, enabling, confused, rigid thinking, fearful of change, complacent and fearful of the forces of Nature and the Elements.

Fourth Dimension (Sub-Planes One Through Three) – Human/Human Kingdom. Human Beings within this stage of evolvement are still using some of their animal instinctual nature, along with the subconscious/conscious human nature. The Fourth Dimension is the realm of emotions and Maya (illusion), the Astral Plane, sometimes called the Etheric Realm. This is the 'place' where our consciousness goes to during sleep; it is also to where we return after death of the physical body and where we incarnate from for another physical lifetime of learning. Since this Dimension is the beginning stage of higher frequency patterns, time is more fluid, and the laws of time and space begin to change. Additionally, we must pass beyond the mass consciousness belief structures, which are mostly comprised of a conglomeration of inharmonious Third/Fourth-Dimensional vibrations, in order to leave the Fourth Dimensional realms and tap into the higher Fifth-Dimensional environment.

Fourth Dimension (Sub-Planes Four Through Seven) – Human/Spirit Kingdom. These levels of the Fourth Dimension are characterized by an increasing individual effort and focus on developing the attributes of self-less service to others, rather than living in a "what's in it for me" mentality. Prevailing negative attributes to be overcome or released before ascending in consciousness from the Fourth "up" into the Fifth Dimension include: I-Me-My focus, blame, anxiety, demanding, hopeless, judgmental, destructive, stubborn, materialistic, frivolous, pessimistic, unworthiness, plodding, caught up in mass consciousness belief systems, vain, possessive and lethargic.

Alternatively, positive attributes that must be integrated include: optimistic, understanding, self-discipline, seeking knowledge, insightful, generous, helpful, expanding self-awareness, forgiveness, compassionate, trusting, patient, expressive, creative, merciful, harmonious, serene, courageous, empowering, reverent, loving, joyful, intuitive, gracious, thankful, altruistic, truthful, grateful and having a desire to serve others.

An individual must clear or release more than half of their negative frequency patterns and attune themselves to at least a portion of the lower sub-level frequencies of the Fifth Dimension in order to recall and begin using a portion of your innate spiritual abilities, such as using telepathy to communicate instead of a spoken language. Therefore, a 'visit' to your Spiritual Area requires that you at least temporarily release those energies and feelings that would hold you back.

Fifth Dimension – Unity Consciousness. Humans who have moved beyond the negative attributes of the Fourth Dimension and have a majority (at least 51%) of their energetic expression reflecting the above positive attributes have begun to live in the Fifth Dimension. They have evolved to this level of living in unity and harmony with others of similar vibration. Beginning with the Fifth Dimension, duality and polarity cease to be governing characteristics, and competition with others for recognition, status or resources is replaced by cooperation with others; beings at this level and above work toward the greater good of all concerned, rather than hoarding or hiding resources or seeking power of any sort over any other being. Reintegration of all Third and Fourth-Dimensional Soul Fragments has been accomplished; therefore, the Soul-infused Personality is released from the Wheel of Karma, along with the necessity to again reincarnate into a Third or Fourth-Dimensional body. Continual, but gradual, development of the Superconscious Mind and its intuitive, telepathic abilities is experienced.

There are even 'higher' Dimensions of Consciousness where we still have a physical body. Dimensions One through Twelve are called the Dimensions of Form; however, above the Fifth Dimension, our physical bodies become less material and more energetic (higher in frequency). However, these higher Dimensions of continuing spiritual evolution are not of immediate concern for our purposes for learning about Trans-Scalar Healing; it is sufficient to raise your consciousness to the Fifth Dimension to begin developing your natural telepathic communication abilities that you will use for exchanging information with spiritual beings such as Spirit Guides and Angels, as well as with other humans, wherever they are, in the Trans-Scalar Healing technique.

The "Spiritual Area".

Those who have not yet experienced a more expanded state of awareness where they can consciously hold a two-way dialogue with their Higher Self (Soul) and/or Spirit Guide may wonder what it would feel like in their 'Spiritual Area'. This is a personal experience that is unique to each person; however, an indication of what the Spiritual Beings feel when we reach out to them is available in Chapter 12 of my book, "Spiritual Journeys," where my Spiritual Research Group was investigating the Angelic Realms. I asked the Higher Self of one of my hypnotized students to describe the Angelic Realms, and the reply was:

"It is unbridled joy and love. It is the epiphany of experience. It is nearly uncontainable.... All (beings) are deeply and immediately connected to the One That Is All and feel the strength of the unlimited joy. It is overwhelming as a human to feel that joy and excitement, and makes it difficult to function intellectually…. It is so gratifying to see those of you who are willing to make the struggle to expand your understanding and therefore your knowledge and your consciousness." [Endnote 2]

The following Chapter provides the process details that have been developed for the Trans-Scalar Healing modality where the practitioner is taught how to raise his or her consciousness to their Fifth Dimensional Spiritual Area and provide very effective healing energies when not in the physical presence of their client.

Chapter 4

The Trans-Scalar Healing Technique

Our deepest fear is not that we are inadequate.
Our deepest fear is that we are powerful beyond measure.
It is our light, not our darkness, that most frightens us....
As we let our own light shine,
we give others permission to do the same.

- Marianne Williamson in
"A Return To Love: Reflections on the Principles
Of A Course in Miracles," 1992

This chapter synthesizes the information and concepts provided in prior chapters into a single, comprehensive structure for stepping into your own Mastery as a Remote Spiritual Healer who has learned to summon and direct their own energies, as well as the energies of the Spiritual Realms for the greatest benefit of their clients. The processes and procedures discussed below are those that I have found to be very effective for enabling higher dimensional healing energies to be brought to all energetic levels of a client; however, I encourage each reader to use these words as a starting point for development of additional modifications or adaptations that may be more appropriate or useful for your own particular healing style. The bolded words in quotes are to be spoken out loud by the healing practitioner.

Arranging The Healing Session

Although you may wish to do so, I do not advertise my healing services anywhere except on my website, www.howardbatie.com, and now in this book. The Trans-Scalar Healing page on my website discusses this technique and provides a link to a Trans-

Scalar Healing Session Order Form that can be downloaded, filled out and returned to me either by email or regular postal mail. Upon receipt of the Session Order Form and pre-payment through PayPal, either by direct funds transfer or by credit/debit card, all that remains to be done is to schedule a time that is mutually convenient to conduct the session; normally this is done by direct email contact. As stated on the Order Form, I prefer that the prospective client NOT inform me prior to the session of any physical, emotional, mental or spiritual condition that they are concerned about; the less I know about their condition or situation, the smoother the session information will flow. Additionally, not knowing anything about the client, except their name and the physical address where they will be located at during the session, requires that I remain open to the intuitive information I receive for them, and learn to trust that information completely.

Preparing The Client

At the agreed time for the session to begin, I normally telephone the client (if in the U.S. or Canada) to confirm they are also ready and relaxed, and then ask them to continue relaxing and take notes until I called them again at the completion of the remote session. Alternatively, if the client is not within a free-phone-call distance, at the agreed time, I would simply begin my own energetic preparations for grounding, meridian and chakra balancing at the agreed time, and establish my own Bio-Scalar energy field for self-healing. I then move into my Spiritual Area; and proceed through the complete Trans-Scalar Healing process as described below. After becoming very familiar with the energetic and breathing processes, the practitioner preparation time can be streamlined to take about only 15 minutes or so, and the complete TSH healing sequence takes about 30-60 additional minutes, depending primarily on the amount of time spent working in the Healing Room.

Both you and your client will have the most beneficial healing experience if you, the practitioner, don't consciously know what your client's specific issue or condition consists of, as that would cause you to focus only on that particular disease, symptom or condition, and might limit a much more general healing result. I have found through personal experience that if I don't know about their Arthritis, or about their Cancer or any other condition they have, then I can remain free to mentally focus only on whatever is in their highest and best good for increasing their overall health and wellness.

I really prefer to know only their name and the physical address where they will be located at during the session. I ask them to find a comfortable and relaxing chair – a recliner is ideal. If they use a sofa or bed, I ask them to prop up their shoulders, head and neck up so they're relaxed, but not so relaxed that they might go to sleep. I also ask them to remain very aware of what they sense, feel or become aware of during the session and jot it down, along with the time they felt it, since we will exchange notes after the session is concluded. Although I have also found that notes from the majority of my remote healing clients have not been very detailed, occasionally we are both pleasantly surprised at the synchronicity of our separate detailed reports, as stated the following unsolicited testimonial:

> Your (Remote Trans-Scalar Healing) report is very validating. The overlap in terms of the physical sensations I was feeling display an uncanny overlap. Moreover, I feel a very strong resonance with (your report) of the heart and brow chakras, particularly the former, in terms of the fact that a 'metal net was to shield me from either giving or receiving love from others *and from myself*.' That brought tears to my eyes. Seriously, that is almost the sum total of my biggest struggle. Maybe now I can begin building and expanding on the healing session. It is clear that your work is such a labor of love. Thank you!" -- S.E., Goleta, CA

Preparing The Practitioner

Protecting Your Aura. Any time you are working with or in the energy field of another person, it is always a good idea to create a shield around yourself so that only positive energies are allowed to enter your healing area and your own energy field. This can easily be done just by stating **out loud** the simple prayer that has been given to us by the Brotherhood of Light:

> **"Dear Mother/Father/God, One Infinite Creator, Great Spirit** (or whatever represents the One Infinite Creator to you), **please join me in this Remote Trans-Scalar Healing session for** (client's Name) **in** (city/state/country). **Dear Ascended Masters, Guides and Angels, please join me in this healing session. Dear Brothers and Sisters of the Brotherhood of Light, please join me in this healing session. Dear Higher Self, please join me to guide and lead this Remote Trans-Scalar Healing session for** (name of client). **Thank You! Thank You! Thank You!"**

Clearing Your Energetic Negativity. A combination of breathing exercises and visualization techniques is used for establishing a positive grounding connection with Mother Earth and also for clearing your energetic meridian system. Of all the exercises that I've reviewed, the simplest and most effective grounding technique is the breathing exercise developed by Dr. Valerie Hunt for her "Bio-Scalar" technique for initial preparation of the practitioner. This is then followed by 'The Circle of Grace' for clearing and balancing the meridian system; this process was given by the Brotherhood of Light to their messenger, Edna Frankel, and is used here with her permission. [Endnote 1] This breathing and visualization exercise grounds you firmly to Mother Earth and clears energetic negativity and blockages from not only your physical body, but also from your emotional, mental and spiritual energy bodies as well. It also has the beneficial secondary effects of releasing or significantly reducing physical pain and "recharging your batteries" with additional universal energy. It can also be quickly and easily used as a very effective preventive and self-maintenance exercise.

Grounding Your Energy Field. Dr. Hunt's initial grounding process begins by visualizing a golden ball of light coming up from the center of Mother Earth and into the bottom of your dominant foot on the inbreath (right foot if you're right-handed, left foot if you're left-handed), bringing the golden ball all the way up to your dominant-side hip, pausing for a moment, moving it across to your other hip, and on the forced outbreath through pursed lips, moving the golden ball of light down your non-dominant leg, out your foot and all the way down again to the center of Mother Earth. Do this several times until the movement of energy "feels smooth" throughout the entire circuit. If there is not a smooth flow of energy for this circuit, visualize the energy moving in the reverse direction for a few cycles, up into your non-dominant foot and hip, across to your dominant hip, and down your dominant leg. Then go back to visualizing the golden ball of light coming up into the dominant foot again. Continue until there is a smooth flow of energy for about three or four complete breath cycles.

Ensure that you use pursed lips on each forced outbreath in the entire practitioner preparation phase, as this strongly focuses your energies and intentions. A good way to demonstrate this to yourself is to hold the palm of either hand out about 12-15 inches in front of your mouth, take in a deep breath and exhale forcefully while saying "Haaaaaa" out loud. Notice what your hand feels as you breathe on it. Now take in another deep breath, imagine that there's a candle just in front of your hand, and forcibly blow the candle out through pursed lips like you would blow out the candles on a birthday cake; notice the greatly increased force of the same amount of breath when you purse your lips. Your focused breath carries much more energy, and when you imagine what you intend happening as you exhale, your intention is carried out with much more energy.

Clearing The Meridians. The grounding exercise is then followed by a condensed Circle of Grace process for clearing your meridian system. Visualize a golden ball of light moving up from the center of Mother Earth into your dominant foot and all the way up to your right ear on the inbreath (assuming you're right-handed), and then hold your breath while you circle the golden ball of light horizontally around your head going from your right ear to the back of your head and around to your left ear, then to your forehead, and continuing on around again to your right ear, back of your head, to your left ear. Then on the forced exhale through pursed lips, imagine the ball of light, which by now may be discolored to a gray hue after removing some negativity, moving down your left side and out your left foot and again down to the center of Mother Earth. Repeat several times with a new, bright golden ball of light until you feel that all the negativity within you is released and the golden ball of light 'feels clear' as it returns to Mother Earth.

Opening and Balancing Your Chakras. The popular exercise that spins colored energy into each chakra is then used to open and clear each of your seven primary chakras. Begin by imagining that you're standing in front of and facing yourself; then visualize a clock face located on each of your body's seven major chakras, facing forward. For the Root through Brow Chakras, place the clock on the center of each chakra facing forward with the 12 o'clock position pointing toward your head. Continue to imagine yourself standing in front of you, looking at the clock faces; focus first on your Root Chakra. Breathe in the vibrant Red color of apples or a red fire engine, and breathe that red color out forcibly through pursed lips, intending that the red color bring the CLOCKWISE spinning Root Chakra into its natural healthy vibration. Do this for three to five strong outbreaths with each of the lower six chakras, using the correct color as listed below:

Crown	Violet
Brow	Indigo
Throat	Blue
Heart	Green
Solar Plexus	Yellow
Sacral	Orange
Root	Red

For the Crown Chakra, place the clock face horizontally on the top of your head and facing upward toward the sky. Now imagine yourself above your head, looking down into the top of your head, and after breathing in the Violet color, breathe out forcibly through pursed lips, imagining that violet energy spinning clockwise down and into your Crown Chakra. Do this also for three to five strong outbreaths, intending that the Violet color bring the spinning Crown Chakra into its natural healthy vibration and frequency.

Connecting The Opened Chakras. The clear, open chakras will next be balanced and harmonized to bring them all into a "rainbow bridge" of the pure white light from which each of the seven colors originated. After each of the seven colors have been individually "spun" into their appropriate chakras, on the next inbreath, visualize the color Red in the Root Chakra moving upward to meet the color Orange in the Sacral Chakra, exhale strongly to let the red and orange colors mix and blend together completely, and then breathe normally for one or two breaths. On the next inbreath, bring the combined Red-Orange color in the Sacral Chakra upward to meet the Yellow color in the Solar Plexus Chakra, exhale strongly to let the three colors mix and blend completely in the Root, Sacral and Solar Plexus Chakras, and then breathe normally again for a breath or two. Continue in this manner all the way up to the Crown Chakra, and when you bring all the colored energies up and blend them together with the Violet color in the Crown Chakra, notice that your entire energy column connecting all the balanced chakras now begins to glow and radiate outward with the perfect bright white color that they were originally separated from.

Recall that only when all the seven colors equally balance can the color white be produced. Each color must be equal and in balance with all the others. If, instead of white, there is more or less of a specific color to the column of energies, return to the chakra that represents that color and spin it in again. For instance, if the energy column has more or less Blue color than it should, return to the Throat Chakra (Blue color) and spin the Blue color again clockwise into the Throat Chakra with the strong intention that it mix and blend in perfect balance with all the other colors. Continue this process until all chakras are equally balanced and you *see* or *feel* that the energy column is white, with all individual colors in perfect balance.

Connecting To The Soul Star. When you sense or 'see' the color white, on the next deep inbreath, bring that white color up about 8-10 inches above your head and allow it to mix and blend perfectly with the Silver color of the Soul Star, your 8th Chakra, sometimes also called the Transpersonal Point, or the Individuation Point. This is the connection point between the aura around your physical body and the energies of the higher dimensions. Now, on the next inbreath, visualize or imagine the column of white energy connecting all your physical chakras extending upward and joining with the silver color in your Soul Star, and with your focused outbreath, intend that the white and silver color mix and blend completely.

Horizontal Breathing. Now that your personal energy field is firmly connected to the Universal Energy Field, begin the conscious exchange of the energies of love and gratitude. Focus on your High Heart area, and breathe in the love and joy of the Universe in the form of the color pink right into your High Heart in the center of your chest. Hold your breath for a moment as you move that pink energy down to your Solar Plexus chakra, hold it for a second, and on the outbreath through pursed lips, return that energy to the Universe with thanks and gratitude. Continue breathing pink love and joy on each inbreath into your High Heart, and returning thanks and gratitude from your Solar Plexus chakra, your Power Center, back to the Universe on each outbreath. Continue this for several complete breath cycles.

The Infinity Breath Meditation. Soon after the 9/11 event in the U.S. in 2001, Archangel Michael felt that humanity needed additional energetic help that would assist in staying grounded and connected in the face of extreme widespread chaos and anxiety, and he provided, through his scribe Ronna Herman, the energetic breathwork processes called The Infinity Breath Meditation. This powerfully energizing breathwork visualization has been designed to firmly and energetically connect the practitioner's expanding Human Energy Field to the Universal Energy Field.

Begin by becoming aware of all the Unconditional Love that the Universe hold for you personally – completely loving acceptance of you just the way you are with no judgement whatsoever – total and pure Unconditional Love. On your next inhale through your nose, breathe in all that pure Love energy in the form of the color Pink, breathe it all right into your High Heart, midway between your Heart Chakra and your Throat Chakra, and pause there for a second or two. The High Heart is one of the higher dimensional energy centers of your spiritual energy body. As you exhale forcefully through pursed lips, imprint the energies of Thanks and Gratitude on your breath as you return these energies to the universe. Breathe deeply in this Love in Gratitude out cycle for 3-5 complete breath cycles, always breathing in through your nose and out forcibly through your pursed lips.

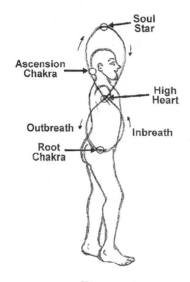

Figure 6a.

Now continue by focusing all your attention on your High Heart area, and on your next inbreath, breathe up through the base of your brain (medulla oblongata, the Ascension Chakra), behind and up over the head to the Soul Star, your eighth chakra, and pause for a second or two. Then breathe out through pursed lips and direct the energy of each outbreath down in front of your face, down through the High Heart, and outward and down your back and all the way down to your Root Chakra at the base of your spine. Pause there for a moment, and then direct another slow, steady inbreath up in front of your abdomen, through your High Heart, up through your Ascension Chakra, and again returning to the Soul Star where you pause again for a short moment. Continue to breathe in this Figure-8 breathing pattern, as shown in Figure 6a. This complete breathing cycle should be repeated for 3-5 complete cycles.

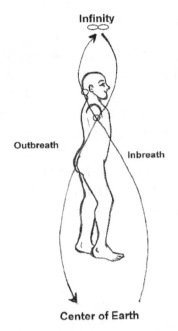

Infinity

Outbreath

Inbreath

Center of Earth

Figure 6b.

The Extended Infinity Breath.

Now focus your attention on your High Heart area and, on the next inbreath, breathe deeply in through your nose all the way up to Infinity and beyond, intending that your entire energy field, including the Scalar Energies you have already developed, expands and firmly connects to the heavens above and the earth below, joining Father Sky and Mother Earth with you in the middle, and pause there for a second or two, feeling the universal connection you have made. Then exhale forcibly through pursed lips all the way down in front of your face, into the High Heart area, out the back and all the way down to the center of Mother Earth, and pause there for a second or two. Then inhale deeply from the core of the Earth, up in front of your legs, up through the High Heart area, up through your Ascension Chakra and all the way back up to Infinity and beyond. Pause for a second or two, and then continue breathing this vertical Infinity Breath for 3-5 complete breath cycles, as shown in Figure 6b, pausing only for a second or two at the top and at the bottom of each breath, while intending and visualizing the connection of all your energies being strengthened and reinforced with each outbreath.

Establishing Your Bio-Scalar Energy Field. Now imagine yourself standing in the center of the universe, and it stretches out to infinity and beyond in all directions to the right of you and to the left of you, in front of you and behind you, and above you and below you. FEEL all the loving vibrations from the farthest corners of the universe in all directions for several breaths. Then,

on the next inbreath, imagine or visualize all these universal energies **instantly** and **equally** collapsing from all the spaces to

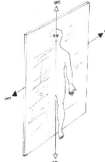

the left of you and from all spaces to the right of you into a thin plane that still contains all the universal love and life-giving energy, and with a sudden exhale through pursed lips, that plane of energy now extends infinitely far out in front of you and infinitely far behind you, infinitely far in front of you and infinitely far behind you, and runs right through your High Heart which is midway between the Heart Chakra and

Figure 7a.   the Throat Chakra in the center of your chest, as shown if Figure 7a. Now breathe normally for a breath or two.

Then, on the next inbreath, imagine or visualize all the universal energies in this thin plane of energies **instantly** and **equally** collapsing from in front of you and from behind you into a thin column of universal energy that forms the foundation of all life in the universe, and with a sudden exhale through pursed lips, this thin column of Universal Love energy now extends infinitely far above you and infinitely far below you, running right through

Figure 7b.   the center of your being, right down through your Crown Chakra, through your High Heart and infinitely far below you, as shown in Figure 7b. Now breathe normally for a breath or two.

Then, on the next inbreath, imagine or visualize all the universal energies of love in this thin column of universal life-force energies **instantly** and **equally** collapsing from infinitely far above you and from infinitely far below you into a very tiny seed crystal of pure unconditional love energy, and with a sudden exhale through pursed

Figure 7c.   lips, all that loving energy of the entire universe now exists within that tiny seed crystal right in the center of your High Heart, in the center of your entire being, as shown in Figure 7c. Now breathe normally for a breath or two.

With your focused intention, you have just created an immensely powerful Bio-Scalar energy field within that tiny seed crystal. This Bio-Scalar energy field has no frequency and does not radiate outward like traditional light waves or electromagnetic energy waves. It is static and therefore remains in the place where it was created. Now notice also that the standing Scalar energy field itself still contains all the Universal energies of pure unconditional love.

Issuing The Self-Healing Decree. Now decree that these Scalar energies repattern your entire energy field. A conscious decree carries much more energy than a simple verbal command; anyone can 'command' something, but a 'decree' carries with it an implicit understanding that the person issuing the decree has the *authority* to do so. With this decree, you are expressing your authority to issue this decree. An effective decree would be:

> **"In the Name of the One Infinite Creator, *I DECREE* that this Scalar energy field now expand into all the spaces within and between every atom and molecule of my physical body and into every frequency and vibration within my entire energy field, cleansing, healing, and bringing balance and harmony to every level of my entire being! *I CALL FORTH* my New Ascended Human Energetic Template, and *I DECREE* that all strands of my DNA be *RECREATED* and *ACTIVATED*! *I CLAIM* the highest degree of physical, emotional, mental and spiritual health that is appropriate for me, consistent with my own soul contracts and chosen life purpose, and ask that all aspects of my entire being be completely filled with Love, Light and Universal Life Force Energy! So be it! And so, it is! Thank You! Thank You! Thank You!"**

At this point, you have performed a very powerful self-healing process, and you can pause for as long as you feel appropriate to enjoy the living presence of this Scalar Energy field. Additionally, you have also done a lot of intentional visualization with these deep breathing exercises, and are probably in at least a light to medium altered state of mind, and possibly in a highly altered state of spiritual consciousness.

The Spiritual Area

As you begin to learn how to expand your conscious awareness into your Fifth-Dimensional Spiritual Area, it's very important that you remain consciously aware of the entire process so that you can direct the guided visualization, while at the same time allowing yourself to become aware of the telepathic communications from your client's Higher Self, and from the White Light Angels whom you will be directing. In essence, you will be learning how to 'walk in two worlds at the same time' with one foot in the physical world and one foot in the Spiritual/Energetic realms.

Access Your "Spiritual Area". The following exercises powerfully combine deep breathing and intentional visualization to expand your awareness into three higher and very specific levels of awareness. These levels have been specifically chosen, as they are analogous to the energies contained in the three higher energy bodies that surround the physical body: the emotional, mental and spiritual energy bodies shown in Figure 5 above. With three successive, deep inbreaths, you will move your conscious awareness from the physical world and raise your vibrations and frequencies, first "higher" into your purest emotional feelings, next "rising" even higher into the ideas and beliefs of all that you believe to be true, and finally, all the "up" into a greatly expanded awareness of the unity and oneness with all the higher beings in creation. Between each of these steps you will relax and breathe normally for a breath or two.

This journey into your Spiritual Area is the equivalent of moving your conscious awareness through the higher octaves in the energy bodies of your aura – first into the emotional energy body, then through the mental energy body, and finally into spiritual energy body where your conscious awareness will be that of your Higher Self.

Deep Inbreath One (Emotional Awareness). Focus on the energies and feelings of unbounded, pure unconditional love, complete joy, and happiness that you see in the eyes of a beautiful, smiling baby, your feelings when looking at a stunning sunset, or as you bring the most perfect and deeply aromatic rose up to your face. Now take big, deep breath in and feel yourself move right into the middle of all that love, joy and happiness; then rest and feel those energies move throughout your entire being as you breathe normally. FEEL yourself *becoming* that love, happiness and complete joy. Pause for a second or two; then breathe out forcefully through pursed lips and breathe normally for a breath or two.

Deep Inbreath Two (Mental Awareness). Now bring all that happiness and joy and love with you as you imagine yourself expanding even more now, lifting and rising into an area where you're completely aware of all the ideas, beliefs and concepts that you hold to be true. And with all your attention now on all that you believe to be true, take another deep inbreath all the way to the top, and hold it for a second or two… and on the next outbreath through pursed lips, send all that unconditional love and joy and happiness that you're bringing with you, send it right into all that makes up your truth, and then just rest in silent gratitude for a breath or two.

Deep Inbreath Three (Spiritual Awareness). Now become aware of an even higher dimension of your being, a spiritual dimension even beyond the <u>need</u> for knowing and thinking, where you can just BE -- a much higher dimension where you can freely express the true, spiritual nature of your own being and you can FEEL that conscious connection of unity and oneness with all of creation. On your next deep inbreath, hold your breath for a moment and as you breathe out forcefully through pursed lips, let go of the need for separateness and illusion, and feel that great release as you just let it go. Allow your mind to easily and gently move outward to infinity and beyond, becoming very sensitive and aware of the rhythms and pulsations of all life in the universe. Move right into the loving whole of consciousness everywhere. As you pause and breathe naturally for a few breaths, FEEL the energies of this very spiritual place that you're in, here in your Spiritual Area. Feel the total unconditional love here, feel the happiness, the completeness, the unbridled joy, and the wonderful connection and oneness with all of life, here in your Spiritual Area.

Am I Really There? The first time you practice these three deep inbreaths, you may wonder if you are completely all the way 'up' into your Spiritual Area, or are you only 83% there, or maybe even only 62%. How would you KNOW? You've not been there before, so you can't 'know' how it will feel or what you will be aware of! I had the same worries as I was developing this technique, but my Guide came to my rescue and whispered in my ear, "Play with this! Let go, and stop THINKING! Move into your heart, and *pretend* that you're right there in your Spiritual Area, and you'll be pleasantly surprised!"

Then I remembered from my hypnotherapeutic training that to the subconscious mind, *imagining* yourself doing something is as real to your brain as actually doing it! However, there may be a bit of the conscious mind that still says, "Yes, but you're just *imagining* something again." However, if you consciously *pretend* something happening, you've already given the conscious mind permission to let go and imagine that image or feeling happening without any judgement or "Is-this-really-true-or-not?" analysis or interference. So, I pretended that I really <u>was</u> in my Spiritual Area, and went ahead confidently with the following healing procedures; but it was my remote clients' positive feedback and responses that ultimately convinced me that I really was up in my Spiritual Area. Surely, all these good things that clients reported could not have happened unless I was really there!

Do Three Things. Even though your consciousness and spiritual awareness has now expanded into the lower levels of the Fifth Dimension, you may occasionally encounter beings who are still learning the benefits of cooperation instead of competition (Service to Others vs. Service to Self); therefore, it is essential that your own energy field be protected against intruders or deceivers. As the practitioner, make sure that you do the three simple but necessary things you must always do each time you come to your Spiritual Area: (1) call for Creator's light and love to surround and protect you always; (2) establish a clear channel of communication between yourself and the highest levels of Love and Wisdom; and (3) state your intention that all information you receive be only for the greater good of all concerned. I always say the same short prayer out loud and state my intentions for each healing session in the following way:

> **"Dear Creator, I ask that your Light and Love surround and protect me always. I ask that a clear and open channel of communication be established NOW between me and the highest levels of love and wisdom, and that all information I receive be for the Greater Good of all concerned! Thank You!"**

It is important that you include the word NOW in your request for establishment of a clear channel of communication. When you are n your Spiritual Area, your awareness will be operating in the 5th Dimension of consciousness where there is no past or future "time;" there is only the present "NOW."

Call For Your Client's Higher Self. When you know or sense that you are protected, call for the Higher Self of your client to come forward and be recognized. For example, if I'm doing a remote healing for Sally Smith in Akron, OH, I would say out loud:

"I call on the Higher Self of Sally Smith at 123 Anywhere Street in Akron, Ohio, to come forward and present yourself in a form that I can recognize."

Many times, the street address isn't necessary, but I always like to include it since there may be several Sally Smiths in Akron, Ohio.

Challenge Whoever Appears. Become aware of who or what appears before you. It may look like the intended person, or perhaps it may look like an animal totem or other energy form that represents the client. Always make sure that you confirm that they are working with the forces of Light, and that they are actually the person you're to work with. For instance, if a farmer in bib overalls appears, the first step of this process is to simply challenge them:

"Farmer, are you in service to the Light and Love of the One Infinite Creator - Yes or No?"

Give them no other alternatives for an answer. Intruders, deceivers or dark entities (and there may be many!) cannot say Yes. If they do not immediately repeat back the answer "Yes" without any hedging or hesitation, you can assume they are NOT whom you summoned. In this case, banish them from your presence by saying out loud:

"Farmer, In the Name of the One Infinite Creator, I COMMAND you to leave my presence immediately and permanently. So be it!"

When you command or decree *anything* in Name of the One Infinite Creator, all the universe obeys. Then call again for the Higher Self of your client to come forward and challenge them again. If they readily answer your challenge with a Yes, you can allow them to remain in your presence. The next task is to ensure that they are if fact who you called forth:

"Are you the Higher Self of Sally Smith whom I am to work with today?"

If they say No, you can still be sure that they are working with the Light, so ask why they have come to you today, and receive the information they have for you. Then release them and call again for Sally Smith's Higher Self, again challenging whoever appears. To release them, say:

"Thank you for coming today. You are released to go about your own activities."

If they say Yes - they are the Higher Self of Sally Smith, ask them to approach closer and look into their eyes if they have eyes, feel their energies, and trust what you feel. Their Higher Self is a higher dimensional aspect of your client's physical self, and will radiate energies of love and compassion.

Always, always, always challenge every single being that you encounter each time you move up into your Spiritual Area, even if it is a being you have met and challenged many times before. And don't worry about offending them by challenging them – they sincerely appreciate the fact that you are very discerning about who you allow into your own energy field and interact with. Just be aware that in the higher dimensions, many beings can assume the shape or form of anyone or anything, including a being you've met before.

If you receive additional specific information about them such as their appearance, stance, the way they move, or their personality, be sure to jot down a note with the details so you can pass it along to your client at the end of the session. If it is appropriate, you may also ask them what they wish you to call them by – what their name or vibration would sound like if it could be spoken in the higher realms. Don't ask, "What is your name?" They don't have "names;" instead, they are known in the spiritual realms by the frequency of energies that they radiate. I simply ask the client's Higher Self:

"What name would you like me to call you?"

Use the name they provide each succeeding time that you address them while you are in your Spiritual Area; using their spiritual name (rather than "Sally") makes it easier for you to maintain your awareness in the spiritual realms, whereas calling them Sally may tend to return you to your physical awareness. Briefly open your eyes and write down the name they give you, close your eyes again, and continue the spiritual healing session for your client. Later during the session, if you can't remember their spiritual name, you can quickly open your eyes, glance at the name you have written, and close your eyes again. Reading and remembering are two very different functions, and simply reading the name without having to remember it consciously will not break the spiritual state of awareness you are in.

If your client's Higher Self has presented itself to you in a form other than human (animal, totem, ball of light, etc.), ask them to assume a human form similar to their physical body so you can more easily work with them during the healing you will provide later.

The Temple Of Healing
Next, ask them if they would like to move to their Temple of Healing. Do not automatically assume a Yes answer, because it is very important that *they* choose to do so. Having said that, I have never received a No answer. Also ask them if it alright if you accompany them to your Temple of Healing; again, make sure that you have their permission to do so; however, I have always received a Yes. As the both of you approach their Temple of

Healing, ask them to describe its appearance, or just send a picture to your mind of how it appears to them. Then locate the entrance and guide them through the opening in their Temple, locate the Healing Room, and invite them in. Be aware of the size and shape of the room, the walls and the ceiling. In my experience, the Healing Room has always been reported to be a warm, inviting circular room about fifteen feet in diameter with a bright beam of white light shining down through a circular skylight in the center of a high, domed ceiling onto a beautiful Healing Table in the center of the room. Whatever the size and shape of their Healing Room is, invite your client's Higher Self to rest on the Healing Table's soft, comforting cushions.

Call On The White Light Angels. Ask your client's Higher Self to invite their own White Light Angels to come and to assist in preparing their energy field for their healing. Continue this dialogue by asking them how many Angels have taken their place around the healing table, and don't forget to ask your client to thank each and every Angel for coming today, and to let you know when that has been completed. When the White Light Angels enter the Healing Room, I have always observed them descending down the beam of white light shining through the skylight and then taking their places around the healing table, but they may appear in any way they choose.

When you understand that the client's Higher Self on the Healing Table has requested the presence of the White Light Angels, inform your client's Higher Self out loud that they must ask their White Light Angels to assist you in preparing their entire energy field for the healing. Again, it is important for them to ask this of their Angels, simply because the Angels will do nothing for your client unless asked to do so by your client, and then will do only that which is asked. They will not overstep their limits and encroach upon your own free will or the free will of your client.

When you understand that your client's Higher Self has given permission for you to provide an energetic spiritual healing, you will first prepare their energy field by requesting that the Angels provide you with several nets of golden light that will successively remove four levels of negative energies from their aura. (Note: This Angelic healing process is adapted from Greg McHugh's book, "The New Regression Therapy," and is used with his permission.)

At this point, you will begin slowly drawing a net of golden white light four times through your client's energy field from below his/her feet to above his/her head. Open your intuitive awareness so that you can witness and record what happens each time a net is drawn through. If you notice the net getting "stuck" or "jerking" a bit at a certain place on the client's body, or moving more slowly or sluggishly, note where and how that feels to you. When you have drawn the net completely through their energy field, ask the White Light Angels to confirm what you believe has been removed and captured in the net. This is very important information that can later give your client some potentially significant insights as to the causes of physical, emotional, mental or spiritual issues with which they have been dealing.

The First Net – Negative Entities. An appropriate request for the first net would be:

"Angels, please provide me with a net of golden light that will locate and remove any and all negative entities from (Spiritual Name's) energy field."

As you slowly imagine drawing the net of golden white light through the client's energy field the first time, it will draw up and bind any negative "intruding entities" in the net so they cannot escape. "Intruding entities" are beings that have attached to the client's energy field in order to sustain their own existence. A negative energetic attachment is possible when a person's energy field is completely opened, either through extreme physical trauma, especially to the head, or during complete medical anesthesia for surgery. Also, an attaching negative entity might continue to seek revenge for being killed; or another might attach to a living drug addict to vicariously satisfy its own craving for the drug on which the attaching entity overdosed while incarnated.

A much darker form of intruding entities is that of beings who follow a path of darkness and evil, or those who have completely forgotten that they have within them the same seed crystal of God consciousness we all have. They have spent so many lifetimes living a life in darkness, they cannot conceive of themselves as having any "good" qualities whatsoever, so through their own choices, they have cut themselves off from the loving consciousness energy that sustains the universe, and now need to draw their own life support energies from other living beings.

It may take as much as 30 seconds as you draw the net from below their feet to above their head; notice if the net continues to move smoothly, or if it sort of jerks or stops momentarily at any location on her body, and then continues. Each place that the net jerks or doesn't smoothly move indicates a place where a negative entity was discovered and removed from her energy field. After you have drawn the net through her entire energy field to well above her head, ask the Angels to tell you what the being removed from each location was there to do, or how it was intended to affect Sally's physical, emotional, mental or spiritual energies. An appropriate request would be:

Angels, what was the purpose of the being removed from her knees?" or
"What was the being removed from her knees there to do, or to make her feel?"

Continue this discussion with the Angels until you understand why each negative being was in her energy field and what is was there to do. If the information isn't initially clear, simply ask:

"Angels, please explain with more clarity what the purpose of each being was."

When the Angels have discussed all the entities that you know were caught in the net, ask the Angels if there are any remaining in the net that you were not aware of. An appropriate request would be:

"Angels, are there any other beings caught in the net that I did not notice?"

If there are, ask the Angels where they were removed from and what they were there to do, using the preceding dialogue. If there are none, then ask the Angels to offer the intruding beings a choice of completing their return "home" to the Light, or returning to the places from which they came – the Lower Realms. An appropriate request would be:

"Angels, inform each of these beings that they have been *discovered* and *removed* from (Spiritual Name's) energy field, and they can never return to her energies or to the energies of any other being. They have only two choices left: they can return to the Lower Realms where they came from, or they can return home to the Light. What is the choice of each being?"

As you become aware of the choice of each entity, record their choice. You now have a unique opportunity to clear the higher dimensions of not only the intruders who have chosen to return to the Light, but also their followers or underlings, as well as their superiors in the hierarchy of negative or intruder beings. An appropriate request would be:

"Angels, separate all those beings who have chosen to go to the Light and those who have chosen to return to the Lower Realms. Now inform

all those who have chosen to return to the Light that they now have a unique opportunity to invite all their followers or underlings, and all their superiors in the hierarchy of darkness and their followers as well, to return to the Light as well. Send out a clarion call throughout all the dimensions of all the universes and let all negative beings know that the Gates of Light are open if they choose to come with you."

And notice if any additional intruder beings accept this invitation. If so, then ask the Angels to gather and bind together all negative beings who have chosen to go to the Light, and escort them there. An appropriate request would be:

"Angels, protect and escort each of these beings who have chosen to return to the Light with unconditional love, and escort them all Home with great joy and celebration! And then fill all the places where an intruder was removed from (Spiritual Name's) energy field... fill them with Light and seal them with Love."

And now we must remove the remaining intruders who have chosen to return to the Lower Realms they came from. An appropriate request would be:

"Angels, for each being who has chosen to return to the Lower Realms, escort them there now with unconditional love, compassion and caring. And then fill all the places where an intruder was removed from (Spiritual Name's) energy field... fill them with Light and seal them with Love."

The Second Net – Invited Entities. There may also be entities that have become embedded in or attached to your client's energy field that are not malevolent or the "Dark Ones," and who may have either consciously or unconsciously been *invited* by the client into their energy field. Examples of this type of attachment include:

Close Family Members. Depending on how a person dies, their soul energy may stay bound to the earth or to another being instead of going "home" to the Light. It could be that a young mother who has died remains earthbound because she wants to ensure that her babies are cared for and nurtured. However, in doing so, she prevents her own return to the higher dimensions of soul.

Grieving Excessively. It is normally expected that family members and close friends mourn the death of a loved one, but in some cases the grieving period stretches into weeks and years. This continuing focus of one's attention on the person who has died can actually create a negative binding energy that prevents the complete return of the soul to the higher dimensions. This is usually caused by an improper understanding of the soul's continuing process of incarnation and return to the higher dimensions after death of the physical body by those who are seemingly deserted and "left behind".

Unexpected or Traumatic Death. In cases where a person has died traumatically or accidentally before their soul's intended or chosen time, it may be that their consciousness is significantly confused and unaware that its physical body is no longer able to be occupied; consequently, it continues to wander in the astral realms, unable to understand why it cannot interact with living beings. It may come into contact with the energies of familiar family members or with the energies of unfamiliar people with whom they resonate because of similar personalities, habits, addictions, etc. Because of this energetic resonance, it's easy for them to attach to the energies of another, not because of any malevolence, but simply to vicariously be able to continue their habits or patterns through their new 'host'.

To remove all invited beings from your client's energy field, an appropriate request would be:

"Angels, please provide me with a second net of golden light that will locate and identify *(not "remove" at this point)* **all entities that Sally may have consciously or unconsciously *invited* to become embedded in or attached to her energies."**

When the Angels have finished, if there are any invited beings located, ask the Angels who was located at each place in her energy field. You may 'hear' or 'know' that it is a relative or friend of Sally who has passed on, or for example, you may just 'feel' grandmother-energy. Now you must begin a dialogue with the located (but not removed) being, for example, a grandmother. An appropriate dialogue would be:

"(Spiritual Name), is it in (Sally's) highest and best good to continue to hold onto Grandmother's energy and keep her from completely returning Home?"

If Sally's Higher Self recognizes that it is NOT in her highest and best good, ask Sally's Higher Self if she would be willing to now release Grandmother to continue her journey Home, knowing that they would soon meet again. If the answer is Yes, begin by asking Grandmother to forgive Sally for holding onto her energies for so long.

"Grandmother, can you forgive Sally for holding onto you for so long?"

The answer will almost always be Yes. Then it's also important that the client forgive themselves so the forgiveness is complete on both sides. Ask your client Higher Self to do that by saying:

"I forgive Sally for holding onto Grandmother for so long and not allowing her to return completely to the Light."

The other possibility (Grandmother doesn't want to go Home, but Sally is willing and ready to release her) must also be appropriately dealt with. While conversing with Grandmother, attempt to make her understand that she has already died and it is both natural and appropriate for her to return to the Light. If she continues to want to be bound to Sally's energies, ask the Angels to gently and lovingly inform her that Sally's wishes override her own. Then ask the Angels to escort Grandmother to the Light and heal the area in her energy field where they were released from.

"Angels, please escort Grandmother to the Light and then fill all the places in Sally's energies where Grandmother was removed with pure White Light and seal them with Love."

However, if Sally's Higher Self chooses to not release Grandmother or herself, you must honor that choice.

The Third Net – Devices, Monitors & Implants. The darker intruder entities may leave behind negative devices, monitors or implants that cause disease, disruption, or irritation in the physical body or in the higher energy bodies of those they have become embedded in. In one session, a dark intruder entity was released from the client's ankle area with the first net, and a pair of leg shackles, complete with clamps and chain, was released with the second net. When I asked the Angels what these devices represented, and how they affected him in any way, I became aware that, in this case, the shackles and chains were devices to slow the client down physically, keep him in the physical world, and prevent him from progressing spiritually. It is always a good idea to ask the Angels what any devices represent and why they are in that location on their body or in their field. Then ask the Angels to deactivate and remove all negative devices, monitors and implants and return them to the Light. When dealing with devices and implants, be sure to say "Negative Implants" or "Negative Devices" because some implants such as pacemakers or breast implants are not negative; additionally, some devices are designed to time-release medications, and you certainly don't want to interfere with their operation.

To remove all negative devices, monitors and implants from your client's energy field, an appropriate request would be:

"Angels, please provide me with a third net that will locate and remove all negative devices, monitors and implants from Sally's energy field."

Again, draw the net through (Spiritual Name's) energy field, noticing where the net stops or jerks as it moves through her entire aura from below her feet to above her head. Then ask the Angels them to show you each device, monitor or implant that was removed and tell you what it was there to do or how it was to affect Sally's body, mind or energy field. An appropriate request would be:

"Angels, show me the object removed from her (e.g., heart area, right leg, brow chakra, etc.) and tell me its purpose. What was it there to do, or how was it to affect Sally's body, mind or energy field?"

When you receive this information, jot down a note to record it, and then ask the Angels to completely deactivate all these objects and return them to the ones who had left them there. An appropriate request would be:

"Angels, completely deactivate all these negative devices, monitors and implants, and completely remove all that can be safely removed, and return the removed objects to the ones who had left them there. Fill all the spaces and places where those

objects were released from with pure White Light and Unconditional Love."

The Fourth Net – Thoughts & Beliefs. After releasing negative entities, invited entities, monitors, and negative devices and implants, it is also necessary to remove the negative energy of thoughts and beliefs given to your client by others, and are not of their own energy. For instance, if, during any of Sally's lifetime experiences, someone else said to her, "Shut up! You're not worth listening to!" with a lot of venomous energy, that other person's negative energy was splattered all over Sally's energy field. Another example would be if someone told Sally she was ugly or stupid, and Sally believed it; the energy of that thought came from someone else, not from Sally. All the "not-Sally" energies that might still be affecting her in a negative way must also be released. An appropriate command would be:

"Angels, provide me with a fourth net of golden light that will locate and remove all negative thoughts, ideas and beliefs, habits and patterns from Sally's energy field that are not her own and that came from someone else."

Draw the net through her energy field as before, and ask the Angels to tell you the thought form, belief or idea that was removed from each location and tell you how it was to affect Sally's body, mind or energy field. An appropriate command would be:

"Angels, tell me the limiting belief, thought-form, idea, habit or pattern that was removed from her (e.g., heart area, right leg, brow chakra, etc.) and tell me its purpose. What was it there to do, or how was it to affect Sally's body, mind or energy field?"

When you receive this information, ask the Angels to completely cleanse and heal these negative energies received from others and return them to the Light. Simply say:

"Angels, remove all these negative and limiting thought-forms that were given to her by others, heal them with Unconditional Love and send them to the Light. Fill all the spaces and places where those negative thought-forms, ideas and beliefs were released from with pure White Light and seal them with Love."

Soul Retrieval And Integration. At this point in your client's healing process, all negative energies that do not belong to the client have been removed and returned to their appropriate places. The last step for complete preparation of your client's energy field is to return all of Sally's own soul fragments that she may have lost in all her incarnations over all the eons of her existence, and to re-integrate those lost soul parts into her current energy field. For instance, in all her prior incarnations, if Sally ever told someone else, "I hate you!" with a lot of venomous emotion, she just splattered a part of her own energies into the other person's field. These fragments must be located, cleansed, healed and reintegrated into your client's energy field.

Sally has already given permission for the Angels to complete this last step, so the Angels will immediately go out into all the places and all the spaces in all the dimensions of all the universes. The Angels will then locate, cleanse and heal all of Sally's lost soul fragments, return them to her, and, under your direction reintegrate them into her energy field. I ask the Angels to do this step and just let me know when it has been completed, which is almost instantly. An appropriate request would be:

"Angels, now move out into all the places and all the spaces in all the dimensions of all the universes and locate and retrieve all of Sally's lost

energies and soul fragments, and present them to me for my inspection."

You will soon learn how the Angles present them to you for your inspection. They have always presented them to me in the form of quivering, dusty, dirty blobs of energy about the size of an egg, all on a large, shiny silver platter. Regardless of the manner in which they are presented to you, ask the Angels to cleanse and heal each of these lost soul fragments, and to then reintegrate them into Sally's energy field. An appropriate request would be:

"Angels, cleanse and heal all these lost soul fragments with the White Light, and then reintegrate them completely back into Sally's energies, making her energetically whole and complete once more with her own energies."

Choose The Healing Energy. Since the client's energy field now contains only Sally's own energies, her energy field has been prepared in the best possible way for any subsequent healing process or technique. The Angels' preparation work ensures that the healing energies you will bring to Sally will not be deflected or distorted by any negative entities, devices or energies within her aura.

At this point, just after the White Light Angels have completed preparing her energy field, I always ask the Angels what healing technique will be most beneficial for the client to receive. The Angels will always know what techniques you are trained in, and they will also know what is best for your client. The discussion below deals with some of the healing techniques you may be certified in and qualified to provide. It's also interesting to note that, to date, I've never been asked by the Angels to provide an energy healing technique that I was not trained in.

Using Reiki Energy. Several very authoritative and reliable sources (e.g., Archangel Michael, The Brotherhood of Light, the group consciousness Q'uo, Ascended Beings, etc.) have stated that the energy known as Reiki is a pure healing energy from The One Infinite Creator [Endnote 2], and I have been instructed by the Angels to use Reiki in nearly all of my own Trans-Scalar Healing sessions. Initially, I began by imagining myself drawing the Reiki healing symbols on my palm chakras and stating the secret name of the symbol three times, but the Angels interrupted me and said, "No, no, no… you don't have to do all that! Just put your left hand on their Crown Chakra and your right hand on the bottoms of their feet. Now let go, and charge 'em up!" So, with these simple instructions, even a beginning Reiki I practitioner will be able to very effectively provide a Reiki Healing within the client's Temple of Healing if asked to do so.

Using Other Healing Energies. Although certified and trained to deliver a wide variety of healing energies taught through other techniques, only occasionally have I been advised by the Angels to provide a technique other than Reiki. After nearly seven years of developing and providing the Trans-Scalar Healing technique, only twice was I advised to provide energies from another healing technique; once they suggested that I provide Reconnective Healing, and once it was a specific Healing Touch process.

Using Bio-Scalar Healing Energies. Even if you have never been trained in any other healing techniques, you'll always be able to provide the Bio-Scalar healing energies that you developed in the earlier Practitioner Preparation procedures. If you have skipped those steps before you move to the Temple of Healing, you should develop your Bio-Scalar energy field before you move into Sally's energy field in the Healing Room. This allows healing energy to be provided in a different manner than in a formal healing technique such as Reiki.

However, the real purpose of developing higher vibrational Bio-Scalar energy within your own energy field is to first heal yourself to the highest degree that is appropriate for you (a soul choice) and that you choose to allow (a conscious personal choice). The intentional energetic preparation exercises by the healing facilitator establish predominately higher vibrational energies and feelings (such as healing, peace, light, love, etc.) within your aura, and decrease the presence of lower vibrational energies (such as fear, unworthiness, doubt, anger, etc.). The presence of predominately higher frequency energies removes the need to keep the body's physiology in a state of defense (fight or flight), and instead stimulates the para-sympathetic nervous system to physically activate their own internal healing ability by supporting increased immune system responses, reducing blood pressure, and accelerating repair and maintenance of damaged cells and organs, thereby increasing natural health. It has been said many times that to be an effective healer, one has to first heal themselves, as in the old adage, "Doctor, heal thyself first."

With your aura radiating positive higher vibrational frequencies, when you move into the physical or energetic presence of another person, their body's lower vibrational frequencies tend to come into balance with your own through the process of entrainment. Entrainment is defined as the synchronization of an organism to an external rhythm; in our use here, it can be described as the process of bringing your client's vibrational signature into synchronization with your own higher vibrations, thus allowing your client to come into a higher state of health and wellness, if it is in their greater good to accept what you offer.

Regardless of the healing energy provided, notice when you sense that the client's Higher Self has received all the energy that is required at that time. This indication may come in the form of a message from the Angels, an intuitive 'knowing', or a feeling in your hands that the energy is no longer flowing through you to the client on the Table. The next step is to issue the Healing Decree.

Issue The Healing Decree. This is your opportunity to step into your own Divine Spiritual Mastery as a co-creator of healing. This is your opportunity to command the manifestation of the highest level of healing that is appropriate for your client, and with the direct assistance of the One Infinite Creator. We were all created in the image of our Creator as limitless creative beings capable of manifesting with thought energy, so don't be shy or feel you are insignificant. In truth, you are one of the most powerful beings ever created when you invoke the Name and the Energy of the One Infinite Creator. The late Reverend Paul Solomon of Virginia Beach (the 'other' Edgar Cayce) once said, "We are all child gods, growing up to be like our Father." As you ponder these words, also remember what Marianne Williamson has said in her 1992 book, *A Return To Love: Reflections on the Principles of A Course in Miracles*:

> "Our deepest fear is not that we are inadequate. Our deepest fear is that we are powerful beyond measure. It is our light, not our darkness that most frightens us. We ask ourselves, 'Who am I to be brilliant, gorgeous, talented, fabulous?' Actually, who are you not to be? You are a child of God, and your playing small does not serve the world. There is nothing enlightened about shrinking so that other people won't feel insecure around you. We are all meant to shine, as children do. We were born to make manifest the glory of God that is within us. It's not just in some of us, it's in everyone. And as we let our own light shine, we unconsciously give other people permission to do the same. As we are liberated from our own fear, our presence automatically liberates others."

And in the 1996 edition of her book, "Infinite Mind: Science of the Human Vibrations of Consciousness," Dr. Valerie Hunt states:

> "The emotionally appealing humbleness of saying that one is only a channel, a conduit, or an inert circuit is also not helpful in a healing relationship. If your presence assists healing, you are more than a mechanical circuit; you are an important link, you are divine energies manifest. While you can be humble in view of the profound changes which take place, you are dynamically a part of what happens. To

acknowledge that, strengthens you. To be 'merely a channel' weakens you.

It is also important to remember that your objective as a healer is to facilitate the highest degree of healing that is appropriate for your client, consistent with their soul contracts and chosen life purpose. It is NOT to specifically cure cancer, or heal arthritis, or whatever. You are not in charge of, and may not even be aware of, what is in your client's highest and best good – only their own Higher Self is. Their Higher Self may have elected to manifest a particular disease or condition in the physical body so that the conscious mind recognizes the necessity of learning or changing something in their life. To be the most effective on all levels, the practitioner must realize that, regardless of what you *consciously* want for the client, their Higher Self may override those intentions for your client.

When you sense or become aware that the flow of healing energies to your client's Higher Self has slowed or stopped, issue the Healing Decree **out loud** in a firm voice:

"In the Name of the One Infinite Creator, *I CALL FORTH* (Name's) New Ascended Human Energetic Template, and *I DECREE* that all aspects of (his/her) DNA and (his/her) physical, emotional, mental and spiritual health be RECREATED and ACTIVATED to the HIGHEST DEGREE that is appropriate for (him/her), consistent with (his/her) soul contracts and chosen life purpose. *I DECREE* that all atoms of (his/her) physical body, all spaces within and between every atom and molecule of (his/her) physical body, and all frequencies and vibrations of (his/her) entire being be completely filled with pure Unconditional Love, Light, and Universal Life Force Energy! So be it! And so, it is!"

Witness The Healing. After the Healing Command is issued, pause for a moment and wait for a sign or a feeling or just a 'knowing' that the healing energy has in fact been accepted by your client. After about 10-15 seconds, if you're not aware of a significant change in the appearance of your client's energy field, or of them on the Healing Table, state out loud,

"Creator, SHOW ME!"

Take note of any information you receive about the client's new status. "Ask and ye shall receive." That information might be a change that you detect in the way their energy field 'feels' to you, it could be a static or moving clairvoyant visual image that represents their new status, an audible or clairaudient message that you 'hear', or just a clairsentient 'knowing' that the client now has additional higher energies available to them. For example, the Higher Self of one client initially appeared in my Spiritual Area as a strong, warrior woman with a battle axe in one hand, sword in the other, and a leather Viking helmet complete with horns on her head. But in the Healing Room after the healing, she rose up off the table, threw away her battle axe, sheathed her sword, and proclaimed, "I no longer have to fight... with myself!" If, and only if, the healing is positively witnessed by you, the facilitator, then you can state out loud,

"It is done! It is done! It is done!"

This is your acknowledgement that the healing energies have been received and assimilated by the client's Higher Self and will be manifested in the most appropriate way and at the most appropriate time. The healing energies can always be offered, but they must be accepted willingly. And when the healing energies are accepted by the client, miracles can occur.

Regardless of whether the healing energies were accepted by the client or not, then state out loud:

"Thank You! Thank You! Thank You!"

Download The Healing Experience. If the client's Higher Self has accepted the healing, it is in charge of "downloading" these new energetic patterns into the physical body at the appropriate time, perhaps immediately, perhaps later. Ask their Higher Self to provide all the sensations, images, and information associated with their healing to their Conscious Mind so they can be consciously aware of their entire experience.

Additional Healing Sessions. When the healing process is complete, ask the client's White Light Angels if any additional healing sessions would be beneficial to reinforce or complete the healing begun here today. If one or more additional sessions are recommended, ask the Angels what type of healing it should be – Reiki? Acupuncture? Healing Touch? Another Trans-Scalar Healing session? Homeopathic ointments? Get the details, and also be sure to ask when or how often the additional healing session(s) should be done *in Earth time*. Then when the session is over, you can schedule the client to receive the appropriate technique, or if you aren't trained in the recommended modality, you should refer the client to a trusted practitioner who is. Be sure to thank the White Light Angels for all the information they provide.

Planetary Healing Process.
Begin by asking the client's Higher Self if they would like to assist you in a very special and sacred Planetary Healing Process for Mother Earth as well. A suggested query is:

> **"(Client's Higher Self), would you like to assist me in a very special Planetary Healing Process – Yes or No?"**

Client Assists. If your client's Higher Self would like to participate in this process with you, together call on the One Infinite Creator, all the Archangels, the Angelic Kingdoms,

Ascended Masters St. Germain and Kwan Yin and all beings of Light to assist you in opening another powerful channel of the highest dimensional Loving Light, and to provide that energy from Source down through all the dimensions, and into the Collective Consciousness of Humanity on and in Mother Earth for her benefit and use. Also ask that these higher dimensional healing energies continue to be provided in loving gratitude for as long as they are needed. An appropriate request would be:

> **"In the Name of the One Infinite Creator, together we call upon all Archangels, the Angelic Kingdoms, Ascended Masters, and all beings in service to the White Light, to open another channel of the highest dimensional healing Light and Unconditional Love, and to direct this transforming, healing energy down through all the dimensions, and into the Collective Consciousness of Humanity on and in Mother Earth. We ask that St. Germain and Kwan Yin amplify these energies to the highest degree appropriate, and It is our strong intention that these healing and transforming energies continue to flow in loving gratitude for as long as they are needed."**

I have also been instructed by my Guide to include St. Germain's Mantra of the Violet Flame [Endnote 3]:

> **"In the Name of the One Infinite Creator, we send the Violet Flame! Blaze, blaze, blaze the Violet Flame, transmuting all negativity into Light, Light, Light!"** (Repeat nine times, the number of completion).

While repeating this mantra out loud, visualize or imagine Violet Liquid Fire cascading down the healing channel to the Collective

Consciousness of Humanity like a waterfall of violet lava, spreading around the planet and specifically to all those areas and souls where transmutation and healing of negativity is needed the most. When the mantra has been repeated out loud nine times, then add:

"So be it! And so, it is! Thank You! Thank You! Thank You!"

Allow these highest dimensional energies to flow powerfully and strongly surrounding the entire planet, and visualize the healing energies quickly moving into the consciousness of every being on and in the Earth. Pause for as long as you feel appropriate, and when you feel or sense that the flow of higher dimensional light and love has begun to sustain itself, you can thank your client's Higher Self for their assistance, knowing that the connection has been established, and that the highest dimensional healing energy from Source will continue to flow as long as it is needed. Then continue at "Receive A Message And Release The White Light Angels" below.

Client Does Not Assist. If your client's Higher Self does NOT wish to participate with you, call on the One Infinite Creator, all the Archangels, the Angelic Kingdoms, the Ascended Masters and all beings of Light to open another channel of the highest dimensional energy, and to provide that healing energy from Source down through all the dimensions, and into the Collective Consciousness of Humanity on and in Mother Earth for her benefit and use. Also ask that these higher dimensional healing energies continue to be provided in loving gratitude for as long as they are needed. An appropriate request would be:

"In the Name of the One Infinite Creator, I call upon all Archangels, the Angelic Kingdoms, Ascended Masters, and all beings in service to the White Light, to open another channel of the highest dimensional healing Light and Unconditional Love,

and to direct this transforming, healing energy down through all the dimensions, and into the Collective Consciousness of Humanity on and in Mother Earth. I ask that St. Germain and Kwan Yin amplify these energies to the highest degree appropriate, and It is my strong intention that these healing and transforming energies continue to flow in loving gratitude for as long as they are needed."

Then add St. Germain's Mantra of the Violet Flame:

"In the Name of the One Infinite Creator, I send the Violet Flame! Blaze, blaze, blaze the Violet Flame, transmuting all negativity into Light, Light, Light!" (Repeat nine times, the number of completion).

While repeating this mantra out loud, visualize or imagine Violet Liquid Fire cascading down the healing channel to the Collective Consciousness of Humanity like a cascading waterfall of violet lava, spreading around the planet and being consciously directed specifically to all those areas and souls where transmutation and healing of negativity is needed the most. When the mantra has been repeated out loud nine times, then add:

"So be it! And so, it is! Thank You! Thank You! Thank You!"

Allow these highest dimensional energies to flow powerfully and strongly, visualizing them penetrating deep into the core of Mother Earth and then moving into the consciousness of each being on and in the Earth. Pause for as long as you feel appropriate, until you feel or sense that the flow of higher dimensional light and love has begun to sustain itself.

Receive a Message And Release The White Light Angels. As the facilitator, you should thank the White Light Angels and any other beings that are present – such as Spirit Guides, Guardian Angels, Archangels, etc. – for coming today, and then ask your client's Higher Self to do the same. Then ask the Angels if they have a message for client's Higher Self, and ask your client's Higher Self if it is also appropriate for your physical self to consciously know that message. [If it is not, you would not include that information in your report to your client.] When thanks and gratitude for the time together have been exchanged, your client can then release their White Light Angels to go about their own activities. An appropriate release statement would be:

"Angels, thank you for your assistance today. You are now released with love and gratitude to go about your own activities."

In the sessions I have conducted, the Angels have usually (but not always) gone back up the beam of light through the skylight above the table, and any other Angels or spirit beings in the Healing Room have just dissolved and disappeared from view.

The Closing

Return To Your Spiritual Area. Invite the client's Higher Self to leave the Healing Room with you, closing the door behind you, and as you both leave their Temple of Healing, ask your client's Higher Self to turn around, look at it, and notice if its appearance has changed in any way (it nearly always does). Then return back to your Spiritual Area where you called them forth. Once again, ask them to "download" all the information, sensations, images and energies they have received today into their physical body's Conscious Mind so they can clearly remember all the details. Ask them to let you know when that has been completed. If they give you a message, thank them for it, record it in your notes, and then release your client's Higher Self to go about their own activities.

Return To Full Conscious Awareness. When you are ready, take a deep breath, and state out loud your intention to return to full conscious awareness again, clearly remembering all the information and insights provided to you and your client today so that you can document the entire session. Take a minute or two to clearly focus and become grounded again. A handy glass of water is always helpful. Immediately call your client and inform them that you have completed the session, and ask them to forward their impressions and information to you by email or other appropriate method.

Documenting The Session

Timely documentation of the entire healing session is essential to capture all the details and impressions received during the session, and usually starts even before the session begins. I offer the following as an example of the way I conducted and documented one remote Trans-Scalar Healing session with my client, Sally Smith (a pseudonym), a 63-year old woman living at the time in Toulon, France; I was at home near Chehalis, Washington. The client's name and contact information have been modified to ensure her anonymity.

Session Request. An email request for a remote Trans-Scalar Healing (TSH) session was received; attached to the email request was the completed Trans-Scalar Healing Session Order Form which had been downloaded by Sally from the Trans-Scalar Healing page on my website, www.howardbatie.com. The order form provided her full name, physical address she would be at during the session, email address, and her preferred date and time (in my time zone) to conduct the session. Although she also provided her telephone number, I normally communicate with clients only by email if they are not within the U.S. or Canada. For U.S. or Canadian clients, I call them on the phone to confirm that they are ready to begin, and to answer any last-minute questions they may have. In addition, I ask them to remain conscious and relaxed during the session so they can record any sensations, images, messages, etc. that they become aware of, and the time that occurred.

As requested by me on my website, Sally provided no information at all about why she was requesting the session or what her physical-emotional-mental concerns might have been. It should also be noted that the TSH Order Form also provides the client's written permission for me by name to conduct the session and to anonymously share any information obtained during the Trans-Scalar Healing session with the general public. Upon acknowledgement from PayPal that payment for the session had been made, I contacted her by email and we agreed on a date and time to conduct the session.

Recording The Session. Fifteen minutes before the agreed date and time, I began by first energetically preparing myself, as indicated in my hand-written record as the session progressed. The session was documented on a suitable form while the details were still fresh in my mind. The form used for my TSH sessions was created using an inexpensive forms program available at most software outlets.

My form includes some basic information such as the name and physical address of where the client will be at the time of the TSH session, the client's preferred contact information including both email and telephone, date of the TSH session, their gender, and age or date of birth of the client. The remainder of the session form consists of a series of about 23-25 horizontal lines on which to record the time an action was taken by myself and a description the action taken, usually with appropriate abbreviations by the practitioner. As mentioned above, I have found that during the session, I can open my eyes, quickly jot down short notes of what I do, see, feel, or become aware of, and the time it happened, and then quickly close my eyes and continue with the session, without losing that higher state of consciousness. Below is what I wrote down quickly during the session without 'thinking' about it.

12:45 pm Began preparing myself

12:55 Established my Bio-Scalar energy field

12:58 Issued Self-Healing Decree

1:00 to SA – Call HS happy clown N – banish; beautiful goldfish Y Y geisha "Tzar-**lon**"

1:05 TOH Japanese garden, etheric room

1:07 WLA-4; Spir Healers many

1:09 Net 1 – Lower Abd. Angry, pain, distract; throat not free to speak truth; 2→Light

1:13 Net 2 – chest, unborn child – son – back to light

1:17 Net 3 – abd cactus bush; throat candle/died in fire

1:20 Net 4 – throat: "I'm only a servant to men in my life" F less important than M

1:22 Spir phys – heal sewing up

1:23 Go out – few on platter

1:25 Expand Reiki Left-Handed? RH on crown, L on feet

1:27 Issued Healing Command

1:29 Witnessed: geisha becomes Samurai Warrior w/sword

1:30 WLA – more? Y- Reiki weekly until completely healed & without pain.

1:32 PHP? Y honored

1:34 St. Germain; Samurai's sword pointed to M. Earth

1:37 Rel WLA & SP

1:38 To SA msg: "Stand Tall, Stand Strong! What you do now with your life will be the message you give to the world!"

1:40 Return to cons. awareness

The Session Report. From the rather cryptic notes above, it should be apparent that timely transcription of the entire healing session is essential to capture all the information and impressions received during the session. As soon as I concluded the session, I sent Sally a quick email to let her know that I had concluded the session and would begin transcribing my notes. I also asked Sally to do the same, and upon receipt of her report, I would send her my report, and I would not look at her notes until I had completed writing my report; that way we would both be initially 'blinded' to the other's information. I then immediately began transcribing the following report on a letterhead document, which usually takes about two hours to complete. However, in this case, I did not receive her report until the next day, and I then read her report and forwarded my report to her as an email attachment.

Remote Trans-Scalar Healing Session – March 31

Subject: Sally Smith (A pseudonym)
Address: 1234 Anywhere Street, Toulon, France
Reason For Session: Unknown. No prior information provided.

12:45 pm, PDT   I began preparing myself energetically.

12:55   I began establishing my Bio-Scalar energy field within my aura.

12:58   I issued the Self-Healing Decree.

1:00   I rose into my Spiritual Area and called for Sally's Higher Self at the address above to come forward in a way I could recognize her. A happy clown, looking like a court jester, bounced in, but failed the challenge. I banished it as a prankster and called again for Sally's Higher Self to come forward. A beautiful large goldfish about a foot long 'swam' into view; when I challenged it, it sent a bubble up through the 'water' and in the bubble was a "Yes" – it was in service to the Light and Love of the One Infinite Creator, and another "Yes" bubble confirmed that it represented Sally's Higher Self. I asked Goldfish if it would like me to call it Goldfish, Sally, or some other name, and it replied "Tzar-**lon** is appropriate." I thanked Tzarlon and asked it to assume a human form I could comfortably work with in the Healing Room, and it morphed immediately into a Japanese Geisha. [It was not clear to me whether Sally's current lifetime is Japanese or not, but there are certainly many lifetimes of Oriental energy around her.]

1:05   I asked Tzarlon if she would like to come to the Temple of Healing with me, and she said Yes. As we approached, I asked her to describe it to me or 'send' me an image of how it appeared to her, and I 'saw' a well-manicured, tranquil Japanese garden. In the center of the garden was a shimmering etheric building that looked like a strong castle, and we entered the castle and moved to the Healing Room. As we entered the Healing Room, we noticed that it appeared circular, about 20 feet in diameter with a circular skylight in the center of the high domed ceiling. A beam of sparkling silver-white light was beaming down through the skylight and surrounded a Healing Table in the center of the room. She rested comfortably on its inviting cushions.

1:07   I informed Tzarlon that she would have to call for her White Light Angels to come and attend this healing session by preparing her energy field for the healing I would deliver later. When she did so, several Angels and Spiritual Physicians came down the beam of light and took their places around the Healing Table. Tzarlon informed me that four White Light Angels and many Spiritual Physicians were present, as well as a very loving Higher Presence.

1:09   Tzarlon gave the White Light Angels permission to prepare her energy field, and as I began drawing a net of golden white light through her aura from below her feet to above her head to locate to remove any negative intruders or attached beings, I sensed the net "jerk" as it removed an entity from her lower abdomen and one from her chest/throat area. When I asked the Angels what the purpose of the entity removed from her abdomen was, they replied that it was there to create pain and anger that would distract her from moving ahead and doing what she really wanted to do – to grow and help heal others. The Angels also said that the being removed her chest/throat area was there to keep her heart covered and her throat silent so she could not speak of the love and truth that was within her. I asked the Angels to inform both entities that they had been discovered and removed, and they could not possibly return to Tzarlon's energy field; they had only two choices – to return to the lower realms they had come from, or go to the Light. Both entities chose the Light, and were escorted there with much love, celebration and joy by the Angels.

1:13   I then asked the Angels for a second net of golden light that would locate and identify any consciously or unconsciously invited entities who were no longer serving Tzarlon's highest and best good. As I slowly drew the net through her aura, one very small being was located and removed from her heart area. When I asked the Angels to identify the being, they replied that it was an unborn child, a son, who was being held onto through his mother's (Tzarlon's) grief and guilt. He said that he had fulfilled his contact, and really wanted to return to the spirit world. I asked the Angels to comfort Tzarlon and inform her that one day she would again meet that spirit with whom they had that soul contract, and all would be well. As Tzarlon's grief and guilt were transformed into loving acceptance by the White Light Angels, she readily let him go, and the Angels escorted him back home to the Love and Light of the spirit world.

1:17   I asked the Angels for a third net of golden light that would locate and remove any negative devices, monitors or implants that may have been left behind in her energy field by any of the removed entities. A large spherical cactus-like bush with spiny thorns was removed from her abdomen, and a LARGE burning candle was removed from her throat. I had a definite sense that she had been burned to death as a 'witch' in a previous lifetime for practicing advanced forms of healing and energy manipulation that were not understood by others. The candle in her throat was there to remind her that she better not speak of those things ever again, or she would be burned alive. I asked the Angels to completely deactivate all the removed objects, cleanse them with White Light, and return the cleansed and healed energies to the Universe.

1:20   I then asked the Angels to provide me with a fourth net of golden light that would locate and remove any negative beliefs, ideas, thoughts or habits that had been given to her by others and were not her own. As I drew the net through her aura, it "captured" the beliefs of "I'm only here to serve the men in my life" and "I'm less important than a man." I instructed the Angels to completely remove, cleanse and heal these limiting beliefs with the White Light and then return their energies to the Universe.

1:22   I then asked the Spiritual Physicians to go into every cell of every organ and heal what needed to be healed wherever someone or something had been removed from Tzarlon's energy field, and I 'saw' several surgeon's hands quickly and deftly sewing up tissues very neatly.

1:23   The White Light Angels were then asked to go out into all the places and all the spaces in all the dimensions of all the universes to locate and retrieve all the soul fragment energies that Tzarlon may have lost throughout all the eons of her existence. They did so, and almost immediately presented me with a large silver platter of dusty blobs of energy. I asked the Angels to cleanse and heal these energies and then reintegrate them all back into Tzarlon's energy field, making her energetically whole and complete once more and without the distorting negativities of energies that were not her own.

1:25   I asked Tzarlon for permission to extend my own energy field around hers, and she said Yes. I then asked the White Light Angels if Reiki energies would be most appropriate for her healing, and they said Yes. I then connected with pure Reiki energies from Source and expanded my own energy field to encompass the entire space within the Healing Room. When my energies blended and harmonized with Tzarlon's energies, I issued the Healing Command in the Name of the One Infinite Creator.

1:29   The healing was witnessed by me and accepted by Tzarlon as I 'saw' the Geisha on the Healing Table rise and assume the shape and stance of a proud, confident male Samurai Warrior, full of power and strength with his sword in his hand, but also with much compassion and understanding in his heart. The male and female energies within Tzarlon were now balanced and very powerful.

1:30   I asked the White Light Angels if any further healing sessions would be appropriate to reinforce the healing begun here today, and they replied that another Reiki session would be very beneficial in one week, and further sessions at one-week intervals until she was completely healed and without pain. These Reiki sessions could be locally administered to Sally by a properly trained Reiki practitioner.

1:32   I then asked Tzarlon if he (in his present form as a Samurai Warrior) would like to assist me in a sacred Planetary Healing Process, and he readily said Yes, he would be honored to do so. I asked Tzarlon to join his energies with mine, and together we established another column of highest dimensional healing energies from Source, down through all the dimensions, down through our Crown Chakras, and all the way down into the central core of

Mother Earth for her benefit and use, and for the benefit and use of all beings on and in Mother Earth. We both stated our strong intention that this column of healing energy will remain in place for as long as Mother Earth had need of it.

1:34   Together we chanted nine times the Mantra of St. Germain that transforms all shadow into Light, bringing the cascading energies of the Violet Flame down this channel of Light we had established; Tzarlon pointed his sword toward the center of the earth to emphasize the strength and power of this transforming energy for Mother Earth.

1:37   Tzarlon and I both thanked the White Light Angels, the Spiritual Physicians, and all other Beings present for coming today, and then we released them all to go about their own activities. The Angels and Physicians returned back up the beam of Light through the skylight, and all other Beings disappeared.

1:38   I asked Tzarlon to come with me back to my Spiritual Area where I had met him, and asked if there was a message that he, the Warrior, would like me to relay to Sally's conscious mind. The message is, "Stand Tall and Stand Strong! What you do now with your life will be the message you give to the world!"

1:40   I thanked Tzarlon and released him to go about his own activities, and then returned to full conscious awareness.

Howard Batie

Client's Session Report. (Via email the next day, before reading my above report):

Hi Dr. Batie,

I tried to email you after my session last night but kept falling asleep over my computer so I finally gave up. I got up this morning around 5:30, which was unusual for me because I usually get up at least once, around 2 or 3 am, but I slept right through. Had a HUGE coughing fit and was up for about an hour and fell back asleep again, another unusual thing because I usually can't go back to sleep once I wake up (any time after 5 am). Just woke up about 15 minutes ago - yikes! I never sleep this late (it's now 10:15 am).

I'm sure part of my unusual sleep is due to this cold but I also feel your session had something to do with it. My sleep was very solid and good, by the way.

So, for my experience of the treatment, I focused more on physical sensations. I started to feel relaxed (but not sleepy) about 15 minutes before 10 pm.

[Note: The following times in Sally's chronological report have been adjusted for correction of the time zone difference to allow easier comparison of reports.]

12:57 (pm) - tingly, itching sensation in my chest and the tightness I had been feeling decreased considerably. My chest felt lighter and clearer. I enjoyed this sensation for a bit and the next thing I knew, I woke up and it was about 15 minutes later - darn!

1:15 - Vibration in my solar plexus.

Between 1:15 and 1:30 I had small sensations of itching - R nostril, L leg (upper thigh), L temple.

1:31 - R side of occiput tightened just for a moment.

1:35 - "Sensation" at my throat - hard to describe what it was - not unpleasant, but "indefinable"!   :-)

1:36 - Sensation as if a lot of energy was flowing down both arms and out my hands.

1:37 - Slight ringing in both ears.

1:39 - Both wrists itching.

1:46 - Energy throughout my chest area - it felt "lit up" and I felt energy leaving. I didn't cough for the entire session up until this point, and I had been coughing hard all day. Had a "trembly" feeling in my solar plexus, similar to the previous sensation but a little gentler.

1:49 - Pain at R ankle just for a moment. My chest feels more expansive.

1:53 - Burst of energy/light in my chest/heart area.

1:56 - Short burst of coughing.

I wasn't aware of too much more after this - I think I fell asleep again! Will read your report now (can't wait!) and let you know my impressions and feelings.

Thank you so much, Dr. Batie!!

Warm regards,

"Sally Smith"

Client's Observations. (After reading my report)

Hi again,

Wow, that was an interesting session! It seemed that a lot of my physical sensations (the main ones, anyway) correlated with your report, but I experienced them several minutes after you described them. Is this normal? Maybe it was because of the long trip they had to make between Washington and France! :-)

The clown that first appeared made me laugh and I was sorry that she failed the challenge, but I suppose the Geisha was more appropriate (I'm 3rd generation Japanese-American from Hawaii). If I had a healing room here I'd love to have one like the one you described! Sounds beautiful! I think I was asleep for most of the time when the white light Angels and Spiritual

Physicians were working on me/her. I don't seem to have any digestive problems, but if I'm under stress my stomach/lower abdominal areas seem to tense up and I sometimes even feel a muscular kind of ache the next day, as if my abs were working out a lot! I don't consider myself an angry type of person, but growing up in the Japanese culture, expressing anger was never encouraged! Having gone thru a few years of radix therapy, I found that there was quite a bit of it stored in my body. Hopefully most of it is gone and now even more has left, thanks to this session.

I do know that I've been protecting my heart for several years now, especially re relationships. I hope now I'll be more willing to express what I feel in my heart and speak my truth.

I was struck by the little unborn boy you found in my heart. I had an abortion that really broke my heart and I felt sure it was a boy. It was so traumatic for me emotionally that my periods never came back after the abortion (I was 40 at the time). I'm glad he was able to return to the light where he belongs.

I've been told many times and have had memories of being burned at the stake, persecuted, exiled, beaten, killed etc. for doing healing work. I had a very successful practice doing craniosacral therapy and energy work before moving to France, but I have never advertised or had a website and have always been conscious of wanting to "stay under the radar" and even now I find it difficult to describe my work and don't really like to talk about it. How I ever managed to have the practice I did baffles me, because my marketing skills were non-existent and I was always aware that there was fear behind that - of being "discovered" and then punished.

I found it fascinating that I morphed into a samurai warrior! I always wanted to be one!! :-) When I read about him, I recalled the sensation I had of energy flowing down my arms and out of my hands. I think this sensation corresponded to when I embodied this warrior. So interesting!! I used to feel that I had too much feminine energy and wanted to have more "yang" to balance myself, but having been single for so long, I've become so independent and feel I've become too masculine in the sense of doing everything for myself and never thinking to ask for help. Perhaps this session will help balance the male and female in me so they can both be expressed appropriately!

I think many years ago, and certainly as I was growing up, I felt men were more important somehow than women, but I don't think I consciously believe that anymore. Still, the sub-conscious runs the show so I'm glad that belief went out the window with the help of the Angels!

As far as follow up, I don't know any Reiki practitioners here, or any other energy workers for that matter, but I'll start checking that out. I'm very picky about who works on my body or my energetic fields, and I trust the people I've been working with over the years. I have a R.I.F.E. system machine (biofeedback/energy). Do you think it would help if I gave myself sessions on my machine?

I think I covered everything in the report. Thank you again for doing it the same day I asked! Hope my responses made sense and were helpful!

Warm regards,
"Sally"

My Observations. (via email in response)

Hi "Sally" –

Thanks very much for your detailed reports!

You asked about the apparent time lag between what I do and what you feel physically. I've had clients who are right with me to the second, and others who take several days to manifest the changes. Everyone is so unique and individual! But ALWAYS there is eventually a shift or change of some sort recognized, and usually in the area where I or the Angels were intensely working.

In your report, I see a stronger and very definite energetic correlation than just the physical sensations you reported. You have to know that I really go out on a limb and have to trust the information I am receiving when I talk about someone thousands of miles away whom I don't consciously know anything about. The information about your Japanese background was so strong, but for all I knew, you could just as well have been an African lady who had married a Japanese man. The initial large swimming Goldfish, the Japanese garden, the appearance as a Geisha and then as a Samurai Warrior... a lot of Japanese imagery there, and then you confirmed your Japanese heritage. And then to tell someone I don't know about their unborn son, and to have you confirm that as well, is way beyond just being 'lucky' or 'coincidence'! And even the lessening of the constrictions in your chest/heart area (due only to your cold??) and your unusual ability to relax and sleep well. When you look at the bigger picture of what was going on, it's easier to see the many immediate energetic correlations, if not just physical sensations.

But the big question for you now, as you look at that bigger picture, is how will this information point you in the direction of what you really want to do with the rest of your life? By letting go of some very limiting mental-emotional baggage, you now have the opportunity to step out in life (if you choose to) with the energy and power of that Samurai that you've always wanted to be, and perhaps rekindle a desire to brush the dust off your energy healing work, or even expand into new modalities that can help yourself as you help others. Go, girl! Make a difference!

Again, many blessings to you, and may your efforts be rewarded quickly and handsomely! Thank you very much for the opportunity to be of service.

In love and light,

Howard Batie
Chehalis, WA

Brighten the corner where you are!
www.howardbatie.com

Chapter 5

Afterword

Since I began providing remote Trans-Scalar Healing sessions, I
have noticed that my own intuitive abilities have significantly
increased, and I am firmly convinced that this will occur more and
more frequently, not only for myself, but also for anyone who
chooses to actively work with their spiritual helpers, Angels and
guides. By repeatedly bringing yourself into a higher state of
consciousness and consciously conversing with both your client's
Higher Self and the White Light Angels, you will be 'exercising
your intuitive muscles' and strengthening your innate spiritual
abilities to gain information from higher sources. You will also
be building within yourself a much stronger sense of trust in your
own ability to access higher realms of consciousness and to obtain
accurate information. This is especially so if you also choose to
work 'blindly' without any advance information about your client
except their name and physical location. Below, I offer a few
examples from my own experience to illustrate possible ways that
one's own intuitive abilities can be developed and recognized.

In a remote session that I conducted in the early development
process of Trans-Scalar Healing in 2011, I sensed another
presence in the Healing Room in addition to the White Light
Angels, and as I turned around to meet the being, I 'saw' a monk
dressed in a brown robe with the hood over his face. I challenged
the monk, and he confirmed he was working with the Light, but
he declined to offer a name. So, instead, I asked why he was here
today, or did he have a message for me? His reply was simply, "I
am here to observe and to learn." He offered no further
conversation, so I continued the healing session. When I released
the White Light Angels, the Monk vanished as well. About two
weeks later, I was conducting another TSH session for a different
remote client, and the Monk again appeared in the Healing Room.
I challenged him, and again he confirmed he was working with
the Light. I asked him again if he had a message for me, and he

replied, "Yes! Now that you've asked (smile), it would be very good if you would include a Planetary Healing Process in addition to your Individual Healing Process." He then disappeared. After the healing session was completed, I conferred with my Guide, and with his suggestions and assistance, the Planetary Healing Process was included, as described above using St. Germain's Violet Flame of transmutation, which has been an important addition in all subsequent TSH sessions I have conducted. About a month later, the monk again appeared in the Healing Room as I was working with a different client. Again, I successfully challenged him and asked if there was anything else I could or should do to improve the TSH process; he said simply, "It is complete!" He then vanished, and has never been seen or heard from since.

During a remote healing session in 2012 with another client, several months after I had completed the Planetary Healing Process with my Guide's assistance, I sensed that an additional huge energetic Presence was observing this healing session. This Presence felt indescribably 'strong,' and its infinitely loving vibrations were different and much higher than even the White Light Angels, so after successfully challenging it, I invited it to come forward and offer any suggestions for improving the Planetary Healing Process. After a long silence, I understood that no improvements were necessary for the process itself, so I asked this Presence why it had come today; the response was, "I have become aware of this technique and need to witness it so it can be shared within my own universe." I asked if there was anything at all I could do to assist or accelerate the ascension of Mother Earth, and the clear reply was, "Yes! Open more channels!" I thanked the being for coming today, and then felt it withdraw. Stunned for a while, I then continued to close the Trans-Scalar Healing session.

Higher dimensional spiritual sources and helpers do not normally communicate by using words or thoughts, but by sending complete energetic packets of information – including intentions, emotions and feelings – in a single burst of energy, usually as visual pictures or images, and the channel must reliably receive, understand and translate these visual metaphors into spoken words so they can be recorded and transcribed. As an example of this type of exchange, Ascended Lady Master Kwan Yin [Endnote 3] came forward in 2017 during the Spiritual Regression of a client, and provided a huge amount of information in a single instantaneous image of Mother Earth as a beautiful, friendly dog covered with 7 billion fleas, whom she had helped to bring into existence, and gladly continued to support and nurture with her energies. However, the fleas were all warring and fighting with one another, destroying her life-supporting forests, painfully digging into Mother Earth's skin, polluting and damaging her oceans and seas, and even blowing off nuclear weapons that crippled her. This had been draining the life energy from her soul, and she had become so weak that she could barely call for help; yet her compassion and love for these fleas was so great that she would not scratch or shake off a single flea for fear of harming even one of them. All this information in a single instantaneous visual image! Kwan Yin suggested that the healing energies instead be sent to the "Collective Consciousness of Humanity" for healing the fleas, since they were the cause of her distress and the ones who need healing most of all. Gaia's ascension into higher dimensions of consciousness has now been assured, but the issue now is how much of Earth's human population will also ascend with her. Kwan Yin noted that when healing energies are sent to the humans, Mother Earth also receives them herself; so instead, she suggested that additional healing energies be sent to the Collective Consciousness of Humanity at least weekly by individual healers or small groups, noting that it is easier to focus the intention of compassionate healing through a smaller number of healers. She and Ascended Master St. Germain [Endnote 4], have volunteered to amplify the healing energy of St. Germain's Violet Flame as it is directed to heal the Collective Consciousness of Humanity. For this reason, Trans-Scalar Healing's new Planetary Healing Process now includes Kwan Yin's suggestions.

During a remote Trans-Scalar Healing session in 2011, I was to work with a male client who was to physically be at the home of Carolyn, a Reiki Practitioner over a thousand miles from me. I began my energetic preparations at the agreed time for the session to start, and was ready to receive my customary call from Carolyn that her client was prepared and ready, but nearly fifteen minutes went by without a call from her. I tried very hard to focus my attention on the client at Carolyn's address (which I had never seen physically), but I couldn't find him. And then I 'saw' a red Mercedes-Benz sports car with the top down drive up to the curb and stop in front of a single-story ranch style house. A man got out of the car, walked up the curved walkway to the small front porch and rang the bell. The attached garage was on the right side of the house. A few seconds later, Carolyn called me to say that her client had just arrived, and that she would call me again as soon as he was prepared and ready to begin the session. After the session was over, Carolyn confirmed that the client's car was a red sports car, that the walkway to her small front porch of her ranch style home was, indeed, curved and not straight, and that their garage was indeed attached to the right side of their home looking from the street. That was my first spontaneous experience at Remote Viewing.

I hope you will also find that Trans-Scalar Healing launches you on an exciting journey that takes your healing experiences with both yourself and your clients to a new and higher level of awareness. To begin with, I recommend that you first practice the Self-Healing process several times; this will allow you to become familiar with the Practitioner Preparation processes and also to learn how the Scalar energy field 'feels' to you. Then practice taking yourself into your Spiritual Area, moving to the Temple of Healing, and calling on and releasing the White Light Angels a few times. When you're ready to work with others, you may wish to provide an entire Remote Trans-Scalar Healing session for a few selected clients or friends at first, and then ask each one for their frank and honest feedback, then practice again with any new adjustments that you may feel are appropriate. And, when you're ready to really stretch yourself, step into your own Mastery as a Spiritual Healer, put yourself out there to the public, and make this wonderful spiritual healing technique available to your clients!

You may also wish to begin by announcing an introductory workshop that presents an overview of the Trans-Scalar Healing process to the public about what to expect if they decide to have a Trans-Scalar Healing session. Public workshops are great clientele-builders! And if you have a website, be sure to include a page for information about the way you arrange for and provide remote Trans-Scalar Healing sessions.

In conclusion, I offer the processes and procedures in Chapter 4 as a "recipe" or "technique" that, for me, has consistently produced profound healing results on all levels of my clients' being, regardless of where they are in the world. However, you may wish to consider that these procedures are like a set of "training wheels" for your own spiritual healing journeys. Incorporate them into your own healing toolbox of techniques if they resonate with you; but more importantly, allow yourself to experiment and improve upon them as your own intuitive abilities as a remote spiritual healing practitioner grow and expand, allowing you to truly step into your own Mastery as a Spiritual Healer!

Endnotes

Chapter 1:

1. Maxwell, James Clerk, *"A Treatise on Electricity and Magnetism,"* Oxford University Press, Oxford, 1873, Second Edition 1881.

2 . Tesla, Nikola, *"Transmission of Energy Without Wires."* Scientific American Supplement 57:237, 1904.

3. Oschman, James, Ph.D., *"Energy Medicine: The Scientific Basis."* New York, NY: Churchill Livingstone, 2000.

4. Seto A, Kusaka C, Nakazato S, et al, *"Detection of Extraordinary Large Bio-Magnetic Field Strength From Human Hand."* Acupuncture and Electro-Therapeutics Research International Journal 17:75-94.

5. Zimmerman, Dr. John, *"Laying-on-of-Hands Healing and Therapeutic Touch: A Testable Theory."* BEMI Currents. Journal of the Bio-Electro-Magnetics Institute 24:8-17.

6. Sisken, B F, Walker, J, *"Therapeutic Aspects of Electromagnetic Fields For Soft-Tissue Healing."* In: Blank M. (ed.) Electromagnetic Fields: Biological Interactions and Mechanisms. Advances in Chemistry Series 250. American Chemical Society, Washington DC, pp 277-285.

7. Rein, Dr. Glen, Ph.D., *"Effect of Conscious Intention On Human DNA."* Proceedings of the International Forum on New Science, Denver, CO. October, 1996.

8. Rein, Dr. Glen, Ph.D., *"Biological Effects of Quantum Fields and Their Role in the Natural Healing Process."* Frontier Perspectives, Vol. 7: 16-23, 1998.

9. Hunt, Dr. Valerie V., Ed.D., Professional website http://www.valerievhunt.com.

10. Hunt, Dr. Valerie V., Ed.D., Instructional CD, *"Bio Scalar: The Primary Healing Energy."* Malibu Publishing Co, Malibu, CA, 2008.

11. Ibid.

Chapter 2

1. Barbara Ann Brennan, *Hands of Light* (New York: Bantam Books, 1987), p. 40.

2. Ibid., p. 41.

3. Zolar, *Dancing Heart To Heart* (McCaysville, GA: Editions Soleil, 1991), pp. 47-49.

4. For simplicity, I have aggregated all energy levels above the Mental Energy Body into what I call the Spiritual Energy Body.

5. Richard Gerber, MD, *Vibrational Medicine*, Third Edition (Santa Fe, NM: Bear & Co., 2001), p. 163.

6. Brennan, *Hands of Light*, p. 49.

7. Michael Talbot, *The Holographic Universe* (New York: HarperPerennial, 1991), p. 187.

8. Richard Gerber, MD, *Vibrational Medicine*, Third Edition (Santa Fe, Bear & Co., 2001), p. 115.

9. Dr. Eric Pearl, DC, *The Reconnection: Heal Others, Heal Yourself* (Carlsbad, CA: Hay House, 2001), p. 215.

Chapter 3

1. Archangel Michael, *The Five Kingdoms/Dimensions For This Round Of Earthly Ascension* (Channeled Reading through Ronna Herman, February 27, 2016).

2. Batie, Howard F., *Spiritual Journeys: A Practical Methodology for Accelerated Spiritual Development and Experiential Exploration* (North Charleston, SC: CreateSpace Publishing Platform, 2015) p. 98.

Chapter 4

1. The Brotherhood of Light, (Channeled information through Edna Frankel, *The Circle of Grace: Frequency and Physicality* (Flagstaff, AZ: Light Technology Publishing, 2012),

2. Q'uo (a collective spiritual consciousness) *The Essence of Reiki* (Personal reading, channeled through Carla Reuckert, 28 May 2006)

3. Ascended Lady Master Kwan Yin is known as the Goddess of Mercy and Compassion, and, with the Violet Fire, and would baptize children who were brought to her for blessing. Holding them in her compassionate arms, she would mercifully transmute as much of their karma as Cosmic Law would permit. See *"Ascended Masters And Their Retreats"* by Werner Schroeder, published 2005 by the Ascended Master Teaching Foundation, pp. 170-171.

4. Ascended Master Saint Germain is associated with the energies of Transmutation and Freedom, and has given the Violet Flame of Transmutation as a metaphoric image of these forces. Additional mantras given by St. Germain can be found in "*The Law of Precipitation*," compiled by Werner Schroeder and in a CD titled "Use Of The Violet Flame" by Annette Schroeder; both are available from the Ascended Master Teaching Foundation, Mt. Shasta, CA. See www.ascendedmaster.org.

Glossary

Note: The following words are defined as they are used in this book, and not necessarily as they may be defined elsewhere.

Angel – Higher-Dimensional Being who is 'assigned' to an incarnated soul for constant protection and to assist in creating opportunities and experiences in the human's life that will allow them to make beneficial choices in his/her life without interfering with the human's free will. Each human has at least one Angel that works with them. Angels and Archangels do not normally incarnate, but may do so for a few minutes when needed.

Archangel – Higher Dimensional Being whose purpose is to guide the spiritual development of civilizations, planets or galaxies.

Ascended Master / Ascended Lady Master – A spiritual being who has had several physical lifetimes on Earth and whose soul consciousness has ascended above the need to physically reincarnate again, but has chosen to remain near Earth to mentor and assist other humans in their own spiritual ascension process. Examples are Jesus (Sananda), Mary (Mother Mary), Siddartha Guatama (The Buddha), Confucius, St. Germain, Kwan Yin, etc. See *"Ascended Masters And Their Retreats"* by Werner Schroeder, published 2005 by the Ascended Master Teaching Foundation (www.ascendedmaster.org).

Aura – The composite electromagnetic energy field (aura) that surrounds each living being.

Bio-Scalar Healing – An energetic healing technique developed by Dr. Valerie V. Hunt that uses self-generated Scalar Energy. See www.valerievhunt.com.

Chakra System – The system of spinning electromagnetic energy centers on and within the human body that exchanges vital energies with the Universal Energy Field.

Dimension – A state of conscious awareness; specifically, the five Dimensions or States of Consciousness Awareness as defined by Archangel Michael (see Chapter 3).

Emotional Energy Body – The electromagnetic component of the human aura or energy field that contains the patterns or vibrations of emotions and feelings (e.g., love, hate, anger, self-confidence, joy, compassion, etc.). The pattern of energies in the Emotional Energy Body interpenetrate the Etheric and Physical Energy Bodies and is the direct result and reflection of the beliefs and ideas that a person holds about themselves and others in their Mental Energy Body. This pattern of emotional vibrations that one feels about themselves and others is reflected in the both the Etheric and Physical Energy Bodies.

Electromagnetic Energy – Dynamic energy that is propagated at or near the speed of light, depending on the medium through which it propagates, with periodic variations in both electric and magnetic field intensities. Examples include radio broadcasts, x-ray, visible light, gamma rays, etc.

Etheric Energy Body – The electromagnetic component of the human aura or energy field that contains the blueprint or pattern for every cell and organ of the Physical Body. The Etheric Energy Body is an energetic 'double' of the Physical Body.

Guide – See "Spirit Guide".

Healing Touch – An energy healing technique developed by the late Janet Mentgen, RN, primarily for use by other nurses in a hospital setting; however, it is also regularly taught to interested non-medical persons as well.

Hertz – Cycle Per Second; a measure of the Frequency for one complete cycle of electric or electromagnetic energy.

Higher Self – The eternal higher dimensional soul aspect of a person or your client.

Holistic – Addressing the whole being's energy system including their Physical, Etheric, Emotional, Mental and Spiritual aspects and energies.

Human Energy Field – That portion of the Universal Energy Field that manifests as the human physical and energetic bodies or levels. The Human Energy Field is composed of the Chakra System, the Energy Meridians used in Acupuncture, and the physical and subtle Human Energy Bodies. (See Chapter 2)

Life between Lives Therapy – An advanced hypnotic regression technique that allows investigation of the soul's experiences during the interval in the spiritual realms between physical incarnations.

Magnetometer – A device used to detect and monitor the magnetic field fluctuations and vibrations. When used on a human body, it is usually placed on or near the head and/or heart where the human magnetic fields generated by the cells and organs are most prominent.

Newtonian Physics – The scientific study that deals with the interaction of physical matter, energy and gravity in fields such as mechanics, optics, heat, electricity, magnetism, radiation, etc.

Past Life Regression – A hypnotic technique used to investigate and understand the lifetime experiences of a client prior to their current incarnation.

Physical Energy Body – The physical human body's energetic vibrations that can be detected by our organs of sight, sound, touch, taste and smell.

Qi Gong – A Chinese energetic technique used for healing human and animal lifeforms, and also for the martial arts.

Quantum Mechanics - The branch of physics concerned with the fundamental theory of nature at the small scales, and of the energy levels of atoms and subatomic particles.

Reiki – A Japanese healing technique in which the facilitator guides or directs higher-dimensional healing energies from Source through themselves to the recipient, who may be in the facilitator's physical presence or anywhere in the world.

RoHun – An energetic healing technique taught at Delphi University in Georgia (www.delphiu.com) which releases or repatterns all the major negative or limiting emotional energies within the client's aura.

Scalar Energy – A non-physical form of energy that has a magnitude describable by a real number and no direction of motion. Scalar Energy exhibits the non-local faster-than-light characteristics describable by Quantum Mechanics instead of Newtonian Physics (See Chapter 1).

Spirit Guide – A higher-dimensional being who serves as a wise teacher or mentor to an incarnated soul essence throughout the entire existence of that soul essence.

Spiritual Area – An expanded state of awareness that allows a person's Higher Self to consciously interact directly with other spiritual beings.

Spiritual Awareness or Consciousness – The degree to which a being is consciously aware of his or her personal and eternal energetic connection to The Creator Of All.

Spiritual Energy Body – The first level of embodiment and personalization of the Higher Self (See Chapter 2). As such, the Spiritual Energy Body contains the vibrational imprints of the

Higher Self's 'mission' and purpose for incarnating, as well as all the Higher Self's soul memories and history of experiences since its creation.

Spiritual Regression – The hypnotic process of tapping into and consciously retrieving the memories and experiences of the Higher Self's previous expressions as an incarnated human being that are contained within the Spiritual Energy Body.

Subtle Energy – The energetic levels of a person's energy field that normally cannot be seen (i.e., the Etheric, Emotional, Mental and Spiritual Energy Bodies shown in Figure 5).

Universal Energy Field – For purposes of this book, the Universal Energy Field is defined as all the energies in the universe other than the Human Energy Field of incarnated human beings.

Bibliography

Batie, Howard F., *Healing Body, Mind & Spirit: A Guide To Energy-Based Healing.* (Woodbury, MN: Llewellyn Worldwide Publications, 2003).

-------. *Spiritual Journeys: A Practical Methodology for Accelerated Spiritual Development and Experiential Exploration.* (North Charleston, SC: CreateSpace Publishing Platform, 2015).

-------. *The ETs Speak: Who We Are & Why We're Here.* (North Charleston, SC: CreateSpace Publishing Platform, 2016).

Benor, Daniel J., M.D., *"Spiritual Healing: A Scientific Validation of a Healing Revolution"* (Southfield, MI: Vision Publications, 2001).

Brennan, Barbara Ann, *Hands Of Light.* (New York: Bantam Books, 1987).

-------. *Light Emerging.* (New York: Bantam Books, 1993).

Dacher, Elliott S., M.D., *"PsychoNeuroImmunology: The New Mind/Body Healing Program"* (New York: Paragon House, 1993).

Dossey, Larry, M.D., *"Healing Words: The Power of Prayer and the Practice of Medicine"* (New York: Harper Paperbacks, 1993).

Elkins, Don, Carla Reuckert, and James McCarty, *The Ra Material: The Law of One, Books 1-5.* (Atglen, PA: The Whitford Press, a Division of Schiffer Publishing, 1982).

Frankel, Edna, *The Circle of Grace: Frequency and Physicality* (Flagstaff, AZ: Light Technology Publishing, 2012)

Gallo, Fred P., Ph.D., *"Energy Diagnostic and Treatment Methods"* (New York: W. W. Norton & Co., 2000).

Gerber, Dr. Richard, MD., *Vibrational Medicine, Third Edition.* (Santa Fe, NM: Bear & Co., 2001).

Goldberg, Dr. Bruce, *"Soul Healing"* (St. Paul, MN: Llewellyn Publications, 1998).

Gordon, Richard, *Quantum-Touch: The Power To Heal.* (Berkeley, CA: North Atlantic Book, Revised Edition, 2002).

Hay, Louise L., *You Can Heal Your Life.* (Carlsbad, CA: Hay House, Inc., 2004).

Hoodwin, Shepherd, *"The Journey of Your Soul"* (New York, NY, The Summerjoy Press, 1995).

Hunt, Dr. Valerie V., Ed.D., *Bio-Scalar: The Primary Healing Energy.* (Malibu, CA: Malibu Publishing Co, 2008).

Karagulla, Shafica, M.D. and Dora van Gelder Kunz, *"The Chakras and the Human Energy Fields"* (Wheaton, IL: Quest Books, 1989).

King, Godfre Ray, *Unveiled Mysteries.* (Mt. Shasta, CA: Ascended Master Teaching Foundation, 2008).

Kuthumi, Ascended Master, *Teachings For The New Golden Age.* (A channeled work) (Mt. Shasta, CA: Ascended Master Teaching Foundation, 2002

Maxwell, James Clerk, *A Treatise on Electricity and Magnetism,* Oxford Press, Oxford, 1873.

McHugh, Greg, *The New Regression Therapy* (Lexington, KY: Self-Published, 2010).

Newton, Dr. Michael, Ph.D., *"Journey of Souls"* (St. Paul, MN, Llewellyn Publications, 5th Edition, 2001).

---------, *"Destiny of Souls"* (St. Paul, MN, Llewellyn Publications, 1st Edition, 2000).

Modi, Shakuntala, M.D., *"Memories of God and Creation"* (Charlottesville, VA, Hampton Roads Publishing Company, Inc., 2000).

Oschman, James L., *What Is Healing Energy?* (Journal of Bodywork and Movement Therapies, January 1998).

Pearl, Dr. Eric, M.D., *The Reconnection: Heal Others, Heal Yourself* (Carlsbad, CA: Hay House, Inc., 2001)

Pert, Candace, Ph.D., *"Molecules of Emotion: The Science Behind Mind-Body Medicine"* (New York: Touchstone Books, 1997).

Printz, Thomas, *The Seven Mighty Elohim Speak.* (Mt. Shasta, CA: Ascended Master Teaching Foundation, 1986).

Rein, Dr. Glen, Ph.D., *Effect of Conscious Intention On Human DNA.* (Proceedings of the International Forum on New Science, Denver, CO, October 1996).

-------. *Biological Effects Of Quantum Field And Their Role In The Natural Healing Process.* (Frontier Perspectives, Vol 7: 16-23. 1998).

Schroeder, Werner, Ed., *Man - His Origin, History and Destiny.* (Mt. Shasta, CA: Ascended Master Teaching Foundation, 1984).

-------. *The Law Of Precipitation: How To Successfully Meet Life's Daily Needs* (Mt. Shasta, CA: Ascended Master Teaching Foundation, 2000).

Selig, Paul, *The Book Of Mastery.* (New York, NY: Imprint of Penguin Random House LLC, 2016)

Seto, A,, Kusaka, C., Nakazato, S., et al., *Detection of Extraordinary Large Bio-Magnetic Field Strength From Human Hand.* (Acupuncture and Electro-Therapeutics Research International Journal 17:75-94).

Sisken, B. F., Walker J., *Therapeutic Aspects Of Electromagnetic Fields For Soft-Tissue Healing: Biological Interactions And Mechanisms.* Advances in Chemistry Series 250, American Chemical Society, Washington DC).

Talbot, Michael., *The Holographic Universe.* (New York, NY: HarperPerennial, 1991).

Tesla, Nikola., *Transmission of Energy Without Wires.* (Scientific American Supplement 57:237. 1904).

The Healing Revolution. (Life Magazine, Sept. 1996).

Woolger, Dr. Roger, Ph.D., *Other Lives, Other Selves.* (New York, NY: Bantam Books, 1993).

Zimmerman, Dr. John, *Laying-On-Of-Hands Healing And Therapeutic Touch: A Testable Theory.* (BEMI Currents, Journal of the Bio-Electro-Magnetics Institute 24:8-17).

Zolar, *Dancing Heart To Heart.* (McCaysville, GA, Editions Soleil, 1991).

About The Author

Howard Batie

Howard Batie was born in 1939 and raised in Centralia, a small town in Southwest Washington State. In 1962, he graduated from the University of Washington and was commissioned as an Ensign in the US Navy and served shipboard tours of duty in the Pacific during the Vietnam war. In 1970, at the Pentagon, he helped to design and implement the Navy's first satellite communications system serving ships, submarines, and aircraft worldwide. After 20 years' Naval service, he retired as a Lieutenant Commander, and continued to provide systems engineering, technical assistance and operational management support for several military and government communications systems and other overhead assets. He also designed and constructed several custom environmental telemetry systems (Volcano Monitors) for the U.S. Geological Survey; several were vaporized when Mt. St. Helens blew in 1980, and he received national recognition from the Johns Hopkins Institutes in 1981 for development of innovative and practical techniques for using personal computers to aid the severely physically handicapped. In 1995, he left the Washington, DC area and relocated to the Virginia Beach, VA area where he became an energy healing practitioner (Reiki Master, Healing Touch, RoHun, etc.) and a Certified Hypnotherapist specializing in Regression Therapy and Spiritually-oriented Hypnotic techniques. At Delphi University in northern Georgia, he earned a Bachelor of Science degree in Trans-Personal Psychology and, later, a Doctorate in Metaphysics. He authored a series of articles on several holistic healing techniques published in the Virginia Beach, VA publication *"Dimensions,"* and has also authored over 25 general and technical articles published in the computer and electronics fields. In 1998, he returned to the Pacific Northwest and established the Evergreen Healing Arts Center, providing Hypnotherapeutic and energy healing services in Chehalis, Washington. Mr. Batie is the author of **"Awakening The Healer Within"** (2000) and **"Healing Body, Mind & Spirit: A Guide To Energy-Based Healing"** (2003), both published by Llewellyn Worldwide Publications. "Healing Body, Mind & Spirit" was selected by an independent organization as the "Best Alternative Health Book Published in the US in 2003" and was also published internationally. Additionally, he has published **"Spiritual Journeys: A Practical Methodology for Accelerated Spiritual Development and Experiential Exploration"** (2015) and **"The ETs Speak: Who We Are And Why We're Here"** (2016). In addition, he was honored as the 1998 Distinguished Alumnus for Centralia College, Centralia, WA, and is a Past President of the Centralia Rotary Club. Mr. Batie and his wife Anita live near Chehalis, WA, their four children, five grandchildren and several great-grandchildren. His book publications are available at Amazon.com in both paperback and Kindle formats. Go to **http://www.amazon.com**, and enter "howard batie" in their Search box to view his books; his website is www.howardbatie.com.

Notes

Made in the USA
Middletown, DE
10 December 2023

44999370R00076